SATAN, THE MOTIVATOR,

The Battle Between God And Satan

Bishop Roy Bryant, Sr., D.D.

Satan, The Motivator, The Battle Between God and Satan
by Bishop Roy Bryant, Sr., D.D.
ISBN # 0-89228-147-2

Copyright ©, 1999
by The Bible Church of Christ, Inc.

Published by **Impact Christian Books, Inc**. for
The Bible Church of Christ, Inc.
1358 Morris Ave.,
Bronx, New York 10456

Cover Design: *Ideations*

Printed in the United States of America

DEDICATION

I, Bishop Roy Bryant, Sr., D.D. dedicate this book to my lovely wife, **Mother Sissieretta Bryant**, the woman I married on October 11, 1942. She is the mother of our six children and at the time of this writing, sixteen grandchildren and six great grandchildren. On October 11, 1999, we celebrated our 57th wedding anniversary.

You may ask why am I dedicating this book to her also when I dedicated *"Manual On Demonology, Diary of An Exorcist,"* to her. There is a saying that there is a good woman behind every successful man. Well, I am not going to debate that, because in this case, it is true. You may say most men say that about their wives. I grant you that, but, it is a wonderful thing to be able to say it and mean it. God, who is our creator and sustainer, knows that it is the Holy Ghost truth. My wife is a peaceful woman and peace is a wonderful thing. Men have been trying to obtain peace from the beginning of time. As a wife and mother, I don't think there has ever been one better.

Bishop Roy Bryant, Sr., D.D.

IN APPRECIATION

As I move forward in preparation of this manual, I must say that we should never forget those that have labored with us. Therefore, I appreciate Evangelist Antoinette Cannaday, the author of *Out of Me Went 43 Demons.* She has been patiently doing all of my typing.

Bishop Roy Bryant, Sr., D.D.

TABLE OF CONTENTS

PREFACE

The reason I am writing this Teachers' Manual, *Satan the Motivator, the Battle Between God and Satan*, for the serious Bible student, after writing *Manual On Demonology, Diary of An Exorcist*, is that I do not want to stop my writing. Just as Apostle Paul wrote to the church at Corinth in **I Corinthians 9:16:**

for necessity is laid upon me, yea, woe is unto me, if I preach not the gospel.

I find it necessary to preach this, to teach this, and to write about Demonology so that the eyes of humanity will be opened to the works and methods of Satan; to turn them from his darkness to the glorious light of Jesus Christ; from the demonic control of Satan to the power of God.

It was at this time that Evangelist Cannaday, who assists me in the Demonology Classes that I teach in our Theological Institutes and who authored *Out Of Me Went 43 Demons*, was going through my audio material. After hearing my tapes on "Satan, The Motivator," and my other teaching/seminar tapes she became really excited. She then encouraged me to transpose my audio work into written work. What you are about to read is some of my work from many years ago, which is very relevant for today. I have also included some of the most recent studies from my Minister's Training Classes, The President's Research Class (Josephus and Related Studies) and the work from my Demonology Classes held in The Bible Church of Christ Theological Institute.

I recognized how Satan was moving to stop my

ministry. I did not go to any seminary; I was taught by God. I was not part of any church organization, therefore, I can fully understand the words of Apostle Paul speaking to the Galatians:

Galatians 1:11-12
But I certify you, brethren, that the gospel which was preached of me is not after man, For I neither received it of man, neither was I taught it, but by the revelation of Jesus Christ.

When I was first called by God, I found myself not knowing anything about communion. I had no one to sit down with me and point out certain things pertaining to the Scriptures. I was just a man alone with his Bible and his God. The Lord had shown me many visions and an abundance of revelations. I was slain in the spirit frequently. But I did not know Satan.

The Devil has fought me all of my life; even as a young child. At the age of four years old I was hit by a car which left me at the point of death. From the age of 4 to 6, I could not remember anything about myself. I could not eat any solid food. I could only open my mouth enough to receive bread dipped in milk. My mother would let the milk soaked white bread slide into my mouth and down my throat without me chewing it at all. When my memory came back to me, I recall seeing people standing around me. Some thought I would not live, but thanks to God, I survived. I can also recall almost drowning on three separate occasions.

At an early age of 19 my body was afflicted with arthritis. Over a period of time the severity of the arthritis had eaten the tissues out of the lower part of my back. For 14 years it was hell on earth for me.

In 1957 at about 33 years of age, I was healed of arthritis in the late Jack Coe's tent. I entered into the tent as a skeptic, a non believer. I believe that there were about 3,000 people in attendance in the tent. While sitting in my seat, the power of God struck my body like lightening. It went down my spine and knocked all of the arthritis out of my body and God gave me a new body.

Previously due to this infirmity, I could not work without suffering. Many times I was in great pain. It made transportation difficult. I remember missing many stops on the train because it was extremely painful for me to maneuver my body quickly enough to get from my seat to a standing position and out of the door. By the time I was able to do so, the door would close in my face. This is just one of the many reasons why I call this part of my life hell on earth.

I was living good, had a lovely wife, four children (at this time) a beautiful home and a new car, however, I was in constant pain. I swallowed many pain pills and I had a heat lamp on my back. I was strapped in with the doctors wrappings, unable to function as a man and a father should. I wanted to die because the pain was so unbearable. All of these years I worked in pain, continuously, providing for my family.

Finally after years of suffering it was over. After my miraculous healing, I went home and I climbed the big apple tree in my back yard. At the age of thirty-three, I became a boy again. God restored the years that the locust had eaten. This was my first experience with healing. Therefore, I cannot help but praise God for His healings in the wonderful name of Jesus Christ.

Just three months before, I promised God, who I believed in, but, did not know, that if He would heal my body, I would give him my life. It was my neighbor who persuaded me to attend Jack Coe's tent meeting. I did not know in this tent I would find my answer. In my church we did not even talk about healings, the Holy Ghost, or anything pertaining to the nine gifts of the Spirit mentioned in **I Corinthians 12**. I found myself going from church to church still in pain daily. I seen many people in churches that I attended who were in need of healing, but, like me, they were unaware what I found in Jack Coe's tent. Healings and receiving of the Holy Ghost, speaking in tongues, were very new to me.

I can truly say without a shadow of a doubt God has been my sheild and buckler, mighty battle ax in the time of war. King David was a witness to this in **Psalm 23.**

The day that I received the baptism of the Holy Ghost, I believe that I was the happiest man on earth. It was also the first time I heard the Devil speak. He introduced himself to me in a very shocking way. I was attending a small church and at this time the pastor was out sick unto death. I remember a young lady singing the song, "Oh sinner, come home." God stood me upon my feet and by his power I walked straight to the altar and God filled me with the Holy Ghost, speaking in tongues. No one touched me and no one prayed for me. I was very happy, smiling and rejoicing with the people. At last I had the Holy Ghost as the Apostles had received. After the service, I started out to my car. I remember as I was getting ready to enter the car on the traffic side of the street, Satan spoke to me in a very disruptive voice, *"You don't have nothing!!!"* The shock was so great that I stood where I was. I thank God that there was no oncoming traffic at the time. For a moment I thought that this was an illusion. Then, I heard the voice of God and he said, *"Yes, you do. You have the Holy Ghost."*

4

Then I really did smile, even the more. That was my first encounter with Satan. From then until now forty years later, Satan has not changed concerning me and my works. I guest this is one of the reasons that I am an exorcist today. Feeling and hearing this abnormal force was my introduction to Satan. He started with me from the very beginning. However, it taught me something about the Devil that day. He can really be disruptive.

Again the Devil showed up to stop me. Hatred and Jealousy arose in the church I was attending. From boyhood to manhood, I have always been focused to get to the top of my profession. The drive that God gave me as a person turned to a holiness drive. I had a burning desire to serve God; even if it meant supporting the pastor to the uttermost, purchasing food for the saints, cleaning toilets and being a full supporter of the church and the saints. However, the more God blessed me to do, the more it brought about jealously.

I was a blessed man. I owned a beautiful blue and white hard top convertible that many were jealous of. We possessed a beautiful brick home. I had a lovely wife and that time four beautiful children and a good job. I enjoyed coming home from work to take my wife and children to various places. I would say to the family, "Let's go for a drive." We went to the beaches, on trips to our relatives homes, regardless how near or how far away.

Although I had more possessions than those in the church I never thought myself better. You see I was a shy person and a family man. I had no desire to mind anybody's business but my own. However, jealousy turned to hatred and anger. They despised me, renounced me, pulled out and left me. Instead of me leaving the church, they left me. I was called a false prophet and was told that God did not call me.

5

I felt like Joseph when his brothers betrayed him. I do not say it in a boastful way, but a lesser man would have given up.

Never in my wildest dreams did I expect God to take all of me and put me on the path for the ministry. Whatever task God had for me, I desired to do, but being a minister was not one of them. Although God said, *"You will be my minister."* I was reluctant to become a minister or to accept the ministry. However, God continued to show me the ministry. I could not rest day or night. Whether I was in bed, in church or on the job, the ministry stayed before me. One day, I decided that I would pray like Jesus did in the Garden of Gethsemane, "Father, if it be possible, let this cup pass from me." God sent his angels to strengthen Jesus and I thought that this would change the mind of God. There I was kneeling beside my bed at midday in the bright summertime, hoping, praying and feeling trapped with this thing. All of a sudden I felt someone in the room with me. My eyes were closed, yet, I could feel the darkness and something coming down over me as if it were a steel shield about to crush me. I jumped up quickly saying, "Lord let your will be done. Lord, let your will be done. Lord, let your will be done" and I got out of that room quickly.

When God showed me the world at large and what he desired for me to do, to me it was a task far beyond my abilities and knowledge, but, I was afraid to say no.

On November 22, 1959, God fulfilled his word and his purpose in my life: I was ordained a minister of Jesus Christ by a group of bishops and elders of a large organization and a worldwide ministry. They thought that I would stay with their ministry, but it was not to be. I told them my mission, but, they did not accept what I was telling them nor what God had shown me. However, God used this organization

6

to ordain me. After my ordination, they were surprised that I was being led differently than what they were teaching. Why? Because God showed me my ministry. I was casting out demons; preaching a full gospel from **Genesis** to **Revelation** without any church doctrine, but the doctrine of Jesus Christ. God said, "I will teach you the Bible and your church will be different. The name will be *THE BIBLE CHURCH OF CHRIST.*"

All night long, God preached in me "The name of the church will be *The Bible Church of Christ.*" Whether I was asleep or awake it did not matter. He preached in my belly and I felt it in my soul. It did not stop and here I am.

After *The Bible Church of Christ* was chartered, my first church was no one but my wife, four children and my brother-in-law in my living room. Satan even fought me because the first church was in my home. "Aren't you embarrassed because you have a church in your house, What will people think? Today, The Bible Church of Christ, Inc. is a world wide ministry.

I started praying for many of the sick in the hospitals of the city of New York. By the gift of laying on of hands, many were healed, filled with the Holy Ghost, and were released from the Hospitals. I can honestly say that The 1st Bible Church of Christ was built out of the hospitals. Those that were healed and filled with the Holy Ghost began to come to the church through my hospital ministry.

Such it was with a very sick female patient in VanEtten Hospital in New York. One of our great missionaries, Sister Mary Smith, (now known as Sister Mary Parker) requested that I visit with a young lady in VanEtten. This lady wanted me to pray for her healing. I told her to tell the young lady, "If God tells me to go, then I will go." About two days later, the Lord said to me, "Remember the lady Sister Smith told

7

you about; go and pray for her healing." I told Sister Smith, the Lord told me to go. When I arrived at the hospital, I saw this sad lady in pain and on complete bed rest. She told me that she had Tuberculosis of the Spine. I was surprised, because I had seen and prayed for many people with Tuberculosis of the lungs, but not of the spine, so far as I know. God healed many of them; some went home and others came to the many classes I held in the hospitals.

After ministering to this young lady, I laid hands upon her and rebuked that spirit of affliction. The power of God shot through her body and I knew she was healed. After she left the hospital healed, with other of our missionaries I visited her at her home. I again laid hands on her; this time for the baptism of the Holy Ghost. She received the Holy Ghost speaking in tongues. She then began to come to the church. On Easter Sunday, she attended church with her young children and I laid hands on two of them. Both of them received the baptism of the Holy Ghost.

I am very proud to say at the time of this writing, that Sister Lucille Crawley, a/k/a Mother\Missionary, Crawley is one of the great dedicated missionaries and mothers in The Bible Church of Christ Organization as well as a faithful worker in the prison ministry. The following is her testimony.

HOSPITAL TESTIMONY
by Missionary Lucille Crawley

I give honor to God who is the head of my life. I thank God for Pastor Bryant, Sr., whom God used to pray for me.

Before I met Bishop Bryant, Sr. I was a very sick patient in St. Luke's Hospital. I had an abscess burst in my body. The abscess felt like worms were crawling in my body and my bowels did not function properly. This caused me a great deal of pain and required surgery. The hospital took cultures and I was diagnosed with tuberculosis of the spine. Tuberculosis of the Spine required that I lie flat on my back. Therefore, I was sent from St. Luke's Hospital to VanEtten Hospital, in the Bronx, New York for complete bed rest

It was at this time that I met Sister Mary Smith, a missionary from The Bible Church of Christ, Inc. She worked along with her pastor, Bishop Roy Bryant, Sr., in his hospital ministry. Sister Smith told me how God had anointed her pastor, Bishop Roy Bryant, Sr., to lay hands on the sick and they would recover and that I, too, could be healed. Sister Smith told Bishop Bryant, Sr., about me. Bishop Bryant then sent word to me; "If the Lord tells me to come, I will come."

While Bishop Bryant was making his daily rounds, one day, in VanEtten Hospital, he came to visit me. It was in 1967. When Sister Mary Smith informed me that he was coming, I told some of the other patients and they came when Bishop Bryant arrived. One of the patients, who wore very thick glasses, came to the room with her glasses. Bishop Bryant prayed for her and then he told her to read a very small print Bible. She was able to read without her glasses. Bishop then left the room. When she realized that she was able to read the Bible without her glasses, she tried to catch Bishop Bryant, but the elevator door closed before she could catch him.

That same day Bishop Bryant prayed for me and rebuked the spirit of affliction and I was also healed. The next day when the doctors did the x-rays they could find nothing. Even the spots on my lungs were miraculously gone. Tuberculosis of the spine would have caused me to be a cripple in the back and shoulders. A big hump is on the shoulder and back and it would have forced me to be stooped over.

When I was discharged from the hospital, Bishop Bryant, Sr., along with some of the missionaries, came to visit me and I received the Holy Spirit in my bed. On Easter Sunday, at The Bible Church of Christ, two of my children also received the Holy Spirit by the laying on of hands. To God be the glory.

Amen.

I conducted classes in many hospitals, continually praying for the sick. Many received miracles. Terminal patients were healed. Those that could not eat, were able to eat. Many received the Holy Ghost. I can say as Apostle Paul said:

II Corinthians 12:7

And lest I should be exalted above measure, through the abundance of revelations, there was given to me a thorn in the flesh, a messenger of Satan to buffet me, lest I should be exalted above measure.

Space will not allow me to discuss all of the many classes of men and women that I have taught in the hospitals of New York. The closest I can come to describing it, is the account of Philip recorded in the books of Acts.

Acts 8:5-8:

Then Philip went down to the city of Samaria, and preached Christ unto them. And the people with one accord gave heed unto those things which Philip spake, hearing and seeing the miracles which he did. For unclean spirits, crying with loud voice, came out of many that were possessed with them; and many taken with palsies, and that were lame were healed. And there was great joy in that city.

The Holy Spirit is here right now and I exercise the gift of laying on of hands for the receiving of the Holy Spirit just as Apostle Paul, Apostle Peter and the Apostle John did. I never had a tarry room. When Jesus told his disciples to tarry in the city of Jerusalem until they were endued with power from on high, he simply meant to wait for the promise of the Holy Ghost which came on the day of Pentecost according to **Acts 2.** Today, we no longer have to tarry, which means to wait, on the Holy Ghost.

Forty years later (at the time of this writing) as I look back on this ministry it seems as though it was impossible almost to the extent that it never happened.

Soon after I was ordained, while I was standing in the pulpit, God told me that **Satan** desired to kill me. As I stood, I cried before the congregation. I could not stop because it became so real. The congregation wondered why I was crying. I told them that God had just told me that **Satan** wanted to kill me. My question was, Why? Why? Due to the fact I had not experienced anything so vicious or so real a threat, I could not understand at the time. As a young person in the Lord we have had many why's? However, the more we grow and develop spiritually, we then know why. The answers come so clearly.

One cannot even imagine the struggles. When people come to me and say ther problems that have had, my heart really goes out to them. Life is not easy, but it must be lived.

Even with our children being in the ministry, great

tragedy struck in our home. My 4th child, Allan Bryant, was full of the Holy Ghost. He conducted our prayer meetings and the reading of the Scriptures. He was determined to be like his father. At the age of 11 1/2, Allan was struck by a car and laid in a coma two days before he died. While leaving the world, my wife was standing by his bedside. Allan lifted his hand and waved good-by. My wife said as he waved, she knew that he was gone. It was a great loss. Quite a few years after, that remained a great trial for the family and myself. Life has dwelt hard blows to the family. Nevertheless, to God be the Glory.

As a young minister, Satan, once known as Lucifer, Son of the morning, the covering cherub, was trying to stop me.. When he attacks he does in so many ways. Just as it was in my case, sometimes, when we go to the doctor, they cannot find anything wrong. However, it is a physical, mental and spiritual attack, brought on by our adversary, the Devil. For example my whole body, except my facial area, was smitten with scabs. It was a vicious attack of infirmity. For approximately 1 ½ years my entire body was afflicted. I knew Satan was trying to destroy and to make me give up. However, at this time, many were being healed from all types of infirmities and the ministry was growing, I remember standing over a bed in the hospital so weak in body, I could hardly stand, As I was praying for the sick all I wanted to do was to get in the bed and rest. I was a man who loved to bathe everyday. My daily showering and bathing would cause the wet scabs to soften. When I would perspire it would burn. I kept hearing the Devil say, "If you would stop preaching you will be alright. Due to my miraculous healing in Jack Coe's tent from arthritis it took me a long time to go the doctor. I felt as if God had healed me before, he would heal me again. Therefore, I did not go to the doctor right away. Finally after more that a year, I went to a group of top skin specialists at one of the chief hospitals. They all gathered around me, yet, they could not tell me what it was. Therefore, I went home the same way that I entered their office. However, God again gave me a miraculous healing.

I was a young pastor preaching the gospel. This particular Sunday God gave me the message on healing.

Isaiah 53:1, 5:

Who hath believed our report? and to whom is the arm of the Lord revealed? But he was wounded for our transgressions, he was bruised for our iniquities: the chastisement of our peace was upon him and with his stripes we are healed.

We had a powerful and anointed service that day and I then told the church that God was going to heal someone today. After the service was over, I went out into the backyard to show how my legs were covered with sores. However, when I pulled up my pants legs to expose the sores, my legs were clean and my skin looked like new. God did heal that day. It was me. I had been afflicted by the adversary, but God healed me Therefore, I would like to say to the ministers, "Don't give up." The attack may be very great. It can be loss of child, a loved one, sores on the body and/or in the body. It may be an attack from people that are against you and your ministry. You may come to a time when it seems as if no one has a kind word for you. But God will bring you through.

Time will not allow me to go into all the that things that Satan tried. Therefore, I am writing that we might see that Satan never lets up. Remember the words of Jesus Christ.

St. John 10:10:

The thief cometh not, but for to steal, and to kill, and to destroy: I am come that they may have life, and that they might have it more abundantly.

As I have written in my other book, *Manual On Demonology, Diary of An Exorcist,* with all my heart, I speak as Jude, the brother of James, in his writings: These are they who will try to stop us.

Jude 18-19:

How that they told you there should be mockers in the last time, who should walk after their own ungodly lusts. These be they who separate themselves, sensual, having not the Spirit.

Apostle John said:

I John 4:1

Beloved, believe not every spirit, but try the spirits whether they are of God: because many false prophets are gone out into the world.

As you read both of my manuals, **Satan, The Motivator,** *the Battle Between God and Satan*, **Manual on Demonology,** *Diary of an Exorcist* and also *out of Me Went 43 Demon*s by Evangelist Antoinette Cannaday, I pray that God might bless you.

14

THE INTRODUCTION TO SATAN, THE MOTIVATOR, THE BATTLE BETWEEN GOD AND SATAN

THE STUDY OF DEMONOLOGY?

DEMONOLOGY
The study, classification and activities of demons; "invading" the kingdom of Satan.

WHO IS SATAN, THE MOTIVATOR?

The Bible calls him "the god of this world" who has blinded the minds of those that believe not.

II Corinthians 4:3-4
But if our gospel be hid, it is hid to them that are lost: In whom the god of this world hath blinded the minds of them which believe not, lest the light of the glorious gospel of Christ who is the image of God should shine unto them.

The Bible calls him *"your adversary, the devil, as a roaring lion, walketh about, seeking whom he may devour."* (**I Peter 5:8**). Satan is also called the *"prince of this world and the prince of the power of the air."* (Read the following Scriptures: **St John 12;31, 14:30. 16:11** and **Ephesians 2:2**.) Satan tried to stop the ministry of Jesus Christ in the wilderness by offering Jesus all the kingdoms of this world. (Read **St. Matthew, Chapter 4**.) Jesus used the word of God against Satan, continually telling him *"it is written..."*

An exorcist, is one who drives out evil spirits, and he must do everything according to God's word. He cannot go beyond the authority that God has given him. No one can

cast Satan and his demons **"back to the pit."** His time is
not yet and he knows it. Let us refer to **St. Matthew 8:29,
31.**

*And, behold they cried out, saying, What have we to do
with thee, Jesus, thou Son of God? art thou come **hither to
torment us before the time?** So the devils besought him,
saying, If thou cast us out, suffer us to go away into the
herd of swine.*

We must learn to rightly divide God's word because the
demons knows their rights. No one can take rights away
from the devil that God has permitted him to have. Even
Jesus could not torment the demons before their time by
casting them back to the pit. The word of God must be
fulfilled. Again their time is not yet, but their time will
come. The word of God supports my statements:

Revelation 20:10
*And the devil that deceived them was cast into the lake of
fire and brimstone, where the beast and the false prophet
are, and shall be tormented day and night forever and ever.*

KNOWLEDGE IS POWER

Knowledge according to the Word of God gives you
power. Ask yourself, "What does God say about it?" When
Christ came, He came to invade the kingdom of Satan. He
also called unto Him his twelve disciples, and later seventy
disciples and gave them power. He sent them out two by
two and they invaded the kingdom of Satan. *This is the
ministry of Jesus Christ* (Read **St. Matthew, Chapter 10**

and **St. Luke, Chapter 10**) This is what demonology and the works of an exorcist are all about. Christ committed this work to the church. The ministry of Jesus Christ, to this day, has not changed. Ministries have changed, but the ministry of Jesus Christ has not: Neither has God's Word changed.

When an individual receives the baptism of the Holy Spirit, he is snatched away from Satan's kingdom. The whole of heaven rejoices when a sinner repents. But this does not stop Satan from trying to snatch that soul back. I remember in one of our deliverance sessions, a demon said to me "*Roy get out of demonology. You are destroying our kingdom. Pray for the people, teach them and lay hands on them for the Holy Ghost (Spirit), but just get out of demonology.*" You may think it strange for a demon to say, "Pray for the Holy Ghost." Yet, it is because the Devil knows that a Spirit-filled Christian can have a demon. If there were no deliverance ministers and if everyone was fighting against demonology, just imagine the state that churches would be in. If I, and other deliverance ministers, do not invade the kingdom of Satan, many souls will be lost to **suicide, homosexuality, depression, fear, lust, witchcraft,** and thousands of other demonic spirits.

THE WORKS OF AN EXORCIST

An Exorcist is one who drives out evil spirits from the body and/or dwelling place. Again, I repeat, an exorcist must do everything according to God's word. He cannot go beyond the authority that God has given him. Functioning in the capacity of an exorcist, one must first have the anointing and exercise wisdom and knowledge. Every deliverance minister should be able to operate in the gift of discernment according to **I Corinthians, Chapter 12.** To "discern" means to be able to tell the difference between the flesh (personality of the person) and the spirit; what is of God and what is of the Devil. Demons can take over the personality of a person and manifest themselves in his speech and actions. If we cannot discern, we will be talking to, and sometimes arguing with demons, and not know it. We must also discern what is of God. Sometimes the Holy Spirit is working through a person and because we do not discern it to be so, we attribute the works of the Holy Ghost to the Devil. However, everything is not God and everything is not a demon. Sometimes it is just the flesh. **(Read Romans Chapter 7:15-25.)** We must discern the difference.

The original Apostles have gone from the scene, but we are continuing their works. For all those desiring to learn demonology and wanting to work in deliverance we offer teaching sessions in The Bible Church of Christ Theological Institutes. Remember the words of Jesus Christ recorded in

St. John 14:12:
Verily, verily I say unto you, He that believeth on me, the works that I do shall he do also: and greater works than these shall he do; because I go unto my Father.

These works are for all ministers. Many people are calling for deliverance from many different churches. My standard question is, "Have you talked to your pastor?" Ninety-nine percent of the time, I know the answer. Which is, "My pastor does not believe I have a demon because I am a Christian, or because I am saved."

To conclude our consideration of **"What is Demonology,"** remember you do not have to a minister to

20

cast out demons, but you must have the baptism of the Holy Ghost because Satan's kingdom is not divided. [1]

St. Mark 16:17

And these signs shall follow them that believe; ***In my name shall they cast out devils;*** *they shall speak with new tongues (languages)*

---

[1] What Is Demonology was taken from *Manual On Demonology, Diary of An Exorcist,* pg. 27, Author Bishop Roy Bryant, Sr. DD

INTRODUCTION TO THE STUDY OF ADAM:WAS ADAM SAVED?

This study is under the heading of Was Adam Saved, Part IV, page 83.

There seems to be a great controversy by theologians, theological schools and the fundamentalists. Many are teaching and preaching that Adam was saved. You hear so many things over the airwaves because there are many types of teachings. I am really concerned and it has very much stirred me up. I have taken time to transpose my audio work into written work to prove to you through the Bible that much of what we hear is heresies. I am not going to tell anybody that I am infallible, but I do know my Bible and often I say to the people, if you make a statement and I can find in my Bible the word that will contradict the statement you made and prove you wrong, then you are just wrong! The Bible does not contradict itself. Our lack of understanding causes the problem, God's word is Yea, yea; Nay, nay and Amen. The Lord unto John The Revelator on the Island of Patmos these words:

Revelation 22:18-19
For I testify unto every man that heareth the words of the prophecy of this book, If any man shall add unto these things, God shall add unto him the plagues that are written in this book: And if any man shall take away from the words of the book of this prophecy, God shall take away his part out of the book of life, and out of the holy city, and from the things which are written in this book.

INTRODUCTION TO THE MINISTRY OF JOHN THE BAPTIST

You will find this study under the heading of The Ministry of John the Baptist, part XIV, page 319.

Another one of the things that I have desired to write about is the ministry of John the Baptist. Throughout this manual, you will find that I have touched on it, however, I find it important to deal more extensively regarding John the Baptist's ministry. So many of our preachers, teachers, scholars, etc., seem to get away from the message of John the Baptist. **But, you cannot understand, or see the plan of salvation, without studying his ministry**.

I advise every preacher, teacher, every baptized believer and, all those who are studying the Bible and desire to know the plan of salvation to study and understand the ministry of this man. It is very important. We know when people say, "You must be saved," or "You must be born again," they are talking about your salvation. My experience has been, that I seldom hear them mention the ministry of John the Baptist. He was the forerunner of Jesus Christ and one of the most important men in our Bible. Jesus attested to this when he made this statement:

St. Luke 7:28.

For I say unto you, Among those that are born of women there is not a greater prophet than John the Baptist: but he that is least in the kingdom of God is greater than he.

Jesus was speaking about himself, when he said:
He that is least in the kingdom of God is greater than he.

23

Jesus is greater than John. I realize that many are saying "All that calleth on the Lord shall be saved," however, what is the word speaking about? As we go to the Scriptures to find out, keep in mind John's ministry, the word, the time, era and what he spoke regarding Jesus Christ.

INTRODUCTION TO
THE STUDY OF THE HOLY SPIRIT

I have included in this teachers' manual a very important part of our Bible. It is the study and the works of the Holy Spirit, which can be found in **Part X, Under the heading of "The Study of The Holy Spirit."**

I have given you much knowledge on Satan, The Motivator, throughout the Bible. However, our victory is dependent upon the Holy Ghost because Jesus said:

Acts 1:8
But ye shall receive power, after that the Holy Ghost is come upon you and ye shall be witnesses unto me both in Jerusalem, and in all Judea, and in Samaria, and unto the uttermost part of the earth.

The disciples rejoiced because the devils/demons were subject unto them by the name of Jesus, however, Jesus said:

St. Luke 10:20
...rejoice not that the spirits are subject unto you; but rather rejoice because your names are written in heaven.

The Holy Spirit gives us authority and assures us of eternal life. He is our salvation. Yet, I find that many do not know the operation of the Holy Spirit. Therefore, what I am writing is not for debate. It is the word of God to teach and to identify the Holy Spirit.

WHO IS THE HOLY SPIRIT?
He is not an "it." He is the third person in the

God-head. Just as Jesus Christ was the word made flesh and dwelt among us, the Holy Ghost has a function. He is the power and the anointing of God that will complete the God-head; the Father, the Son and the Holy Ghost, which are three divine personalities in one. This is what the Bible teaches. As I stated before, many do not know the function of the Holy Spirit. Some feel He is just here to give us some power. He is more than that.

In this study, I aim to go through the Bible and show you the many ways the Holy Ghost functions. I am not writing church doctrine or what you may believe, or any man's opinion. This is Bible, which is the written word of God. I have given you Scriptures that will support all of this teaching because Jesus said:

St. John 5:39
Search the scriptures; for in them ye think ye have eternal life: and they are they which testify of me.

Therefore, if you cannot accept the word of God, then whom am I? However, Apostle Paul stated:
I Corinthians 12:1:
Now concerning Spiritual gifts, brethren, I would not have you to ignorant.

He also stated in **I Corinthians 14:38**
But if any man be ignorant, let him be ignorant.

Apostle Paul did not say these words to be arrogant. He said it because he found many people to be unteachable. I have met them by the hundreds in Africa, the West Indies and in America. If you can and will accept it, we are going to have freedom and joy in dealing with His word. Jesus said:

St. John 8:32.

And ye shall know the truth, and the truth shall make you free. [2]

---

[2] *This study on The Holy Spirit is also available in a   four tape audio series taught by the author, Bishop Roy Bryant, Sr., D.D.*

GOD HEAD

JESUS · HOLY GHOST

7 SPIRITS OF GOD

HUMANITY
(Man-kind)

Lucifer
Satan Demons/Evil Spirits
Cast out of heaven-Rev 12:9

Cast into the lake of fire-Rev 20-10

DEATH

MURDERER · LIAR

Isaiah 11:2
Rev 4:5

Spirit of the Lord
Spirit of Wisdom
Spirit of Understanding
Spirit of Counsel
Spirit of Might
Spirit of Knowledge
Spirit of Fear of the Lord

FRUIT OF THE SPIRIT
Love
Joy
Peace
Goodness
Longsuffering
Faith, Meekness
Temperance

ST. JOHN 3:16
For God so loved the world, that
He gave His only begotten Son,
that whosoever believeth in Him
shall not perish, but have
everlasting life.

ST. JOHN 10:10
The thief cometh not, but for to
steal, and to kill, and to destroy; I
am come that they might have life,
and that they might have it more
abundantly.

ST. JOHN 14:16 & 26
14:16-17 Comforter-Spirit of Truth
14:26 Comforter-The Holy Spirit

ST. JOHN 16:7-11

Ye are of your father the devil, and
the lusts of your father ye will do.
He was a murder from the
beginning, and abode not in the
truth, because there is no truth in
him. When he speaketh a lie, he
speaketh of his own; for he is a liar,
and the father of it. St. John 8:44

Hatred	Necromancy
Anger	False Religion
Fighting Spirit	Religious Spirit
Cursing	Heresys
Judgmental Spirit	False Prophecy
Murder	Lying
Argumentative	Junk Food
Attitude	Anorexia
Girlfriend Spirit	Gluttony
Boyfriend Spirit	Medication
False Marriage	Depression
Divorce Spirit	Withdrawal
Polygamy	Self-Pity
Sexual Abuse	Sensitivity
Pedophile	Despair
Pornography	Paranoia
Oral Sex	Discouragement
Adultery	Self-Will
Molestation	Talkativeness
Homosexuality	Unteachable
Lesbianism	Spirit
Jezebel	Double Minded
Alcoholism	Ego
Nicotine	Pride
Drugs	Unforgiveness
Witchcraft	Fear of Rejection
Clairvoyance	Root of Bitterness
Horoscope	Murmuring
Fortune Telling	Fear of People
Psychics	Nervous Tension
Rebellion	Corrupt
Stubbornness	Communication

DEMONOLOGY WORKSHEET

THE PERMISSIVE WILL OF GOD

THE WORK OF SATAN
Lucifer, God's Creation
Ezk 28:13-19
Satan, Cast Out of Heaven
Rev 12:7-12
Satan in the Garden of Eden
Gen 3:1-7
The Serpent Cursed
Gen 3:14-19

THE FLESH AND SATAN
Adam: the Adamic Nature;
The Spirit of Cain and Abel;
The Spirit of Esau and Jacob

THE STRUGGLES OF MAN AND THE FLESH
Apostle Paul - Rom 7

SATAN AND THE DEMONIC WORLD (HUMANITY)

SPIRITS THAT DRAW HUMANITY
MIND ALTERING SPIRITS
Chemical Imbalance
Despondency
Discouragement
Doublemindedness
Hopelessness
Loneliness
Mental Depression
Mind Blockage
Mind Control
Schizophrenia
Suicide
Tiredness
Withdrawal

FIGHTING SPIRITS
Anger
Argumentative
Corrupt Communications
Curing
Evil Thoughts
Hatred
Hostility
Memory Recall
Murder
Rage
Retaliation
Temperance
Violence

SEXUAL LUST SPIRITS
Adultery
Bi-Sexual
Boyfriend
Child Pornography
Fantasy Lust
Fear of Rape
Fornication
Gay Spirit
Girlfriend Spirit
Harlotry
Homosexuality
Lasciviousness
Lesbianism
Lust of the Eyes
Masturbation
Molestation
Perverseness
Pedophile
Polygamy
Pornography
Promiscuity
Rape
Uncleanliness
Whoredom

SPIRITS THAT ATTACK THE APPETITE
Anorexia
Bulimia
Depression
Gluttony
Junkfood Spirit
Nervous Tension
Under-eating

SPIRITS THAT CAUSE PHYSICAL ADDICTIONS
Alcohol
Caffeine (coffee, tea, soda)
Crack/Cocaine
Drugs
Medication
Nicotine
Pain Killers
Salt
Sleeping Pills
Sugar
Tranquilizers

SPIRITS THAT GROUP WITH WITCHCRAFT
Astrology
Divination
Disobedience
Familiar Spirits
Fortune Telling
Horoscope
Hypnosis
Lying
Mind Control
Necromancy
Occult
Palm Reading
Psychic
Rebellion
Sorcery
Spiritualism
Unteachable

(FALSE) RELIGIOUS SPIRITS
Backsliding
Cults
False Prophecy
False Religion
False Teaching
Hatred of Pastors
Heresies
Hindrance From
Lying
Occult
Reading God's Word
Unteachable Spirits
Word Blockage

PART 1

FROM THE

AUTHOR'S DESK

Chapter 1

YOU CAN HAVE THE HOLY GHOST AND HAVE A DEMON

In the beginning, I said the same thing many ministers are saying today. "If you have the Holy Ghost, you cannot have a demon because God will not dwell in a unclean temple." Therefore, I can readily understand the way many pastors think. But, God showed me something regarding the words "God will not dwell in an unclean temple." Your temple is not unclean unless you do the works that the Devil is motivating you to do. These acts are contrary to God. Yes, you can have the Holy Ghost and have a demon or demons. Evil spirits work in different areas of the body, but cannot be in the belly of a spirit-filled believer. Remember the Holy Spirit is in your belly.

St. John 7:38
He that believeth on me, as the scripture hath said, out of his belly shall flow rivers of living water.

However, demons lodge themselves in other areas of the flesh. Jesus said:

St. Matthew 5:29-30:
And if thy right eye offend thee, pluck it out, and cast it from thee: for it is profitable for thee that one of thy members should perish, and not that thy whole body should be cast into hell. And if thy right hand offend thee, cut it off, and cast it from thee: for it is profitable for thee that

one of thy members should perish, and not that thy whole
body should be cast into hell.

What is Jesus talking about? Demons lodge themselves
in our sexual organs, eyes, tongues, hands and other various
parts of our body and our minds. This is what happens to
the spirit-filled believers. We do not become possessed if
we are walking with Christ. However, if a believer
backslides, or totally turns his back on Christ, he can
become possessed or even become reprobate (read **Romans
1**) An non-believer (one unsaved) can also become
possessed. The word of God explains in:

Romans 6:16:
Know ye not, that whom ye yield yourselves servants to
obey, his servants ye are to whom ye obey; whether of sin
unto death, or of obedience unto righteousness?

Many of our spirit-filled believers today are yielding
their members (parts their body) to Satan. A fleshy walk
opens one up for demonic activity. We have many problems
with ministers, and in our churches because of demonic
activity. As I stated before, I also thought that a Christian
could not have a demon.

THE TESTIMONY OF THE AUTHOR:
DELIVERANCE FROM THE DEMON OF PRIDE

I do not take the word "Christian" lightly, I am
speaking about a spirit-filled believer) However, I learned
the truth when God delivered me from the demon of
"Pride." It was very shocking that this could happen to me.
I was preaching the gospel, exercising the gift of

laying-on-of hands for the receiving of the baptism of the Holy Ghost and for healings. I knew that God was doing the work and not me. However, somehow, I cannot tell how, the demon of pride entered in. I fought and I fasted. I prayed and cried out to God for a lengthy period of time. After having established churches in Africa and different parts of the country, here I was, having to have a demon of pride cast out of me. Pride was in my chest causing the chest area to swell up. Yet, there was much Holy Ghost in the other parts of my body working with great power.

I thank God for Derek Prince, a demonology/deliverance minister. I went to him for deliverance. Both he and his associates prayed for me. I felt myself jerk and my body stiffen up and then the demon came out.

God taught me a lesson. Therefore, I can understand why many ministers have been and are still saying, "NO! A Christian cannot have a demon." However, I know that many ministers need deliverance, because I have cast demons out of many of them in the past. I do not write this to embarrass anyone. There will be many more seeking deliverance, if they become honest with themselves. We can fool other people, but, we cannot fool God or ourselves. Because many do not believe, we have countless numbers of church members afraid to speak to their pastors regarding their need.

This manual is not for debate, nor to put down, or criticize anyone's belief. I have received much criticism, but so did Jesus Christ, the Apostle Paul, Peter, James and John. We will all have to stand before God one day. If any minister continues to argue and hinder God's people from receiving their deliverances, many will continue to suffer.

Every man and woman who knows the Word of God will know that this manual is correct. I have set forth these words in the name of our Lord and Savior, Jesus Christ, primarily that He may be glorified; and also to expose the Devil. Some people honor Satan through unbelief, and discredit demonology by saying, "You cannot have a demon or demons, because you are a Christian." Because this is a heavy burden on my heart, I am going to expose **Satan, The Motivator,** by means of this deliverance manual and God will get His glory.

All that I am exposing in this manual are the various types of unclean spirits. I am not trying to indicate which ones may be causing your problem. However, use this manual for your guide and your teaching tool to better identify spirits you working with or from which you need deliverance.

It may seem that I have gotten repetitious, but there is repetition in this area according to the word of God. One man had over 2,000 demons in him (Legion in **St. Mark 5:1-20**). One man also beat and ripped the clothes from the seven sons of Sceva. (read **Acts 19:13-20**).

I recommend you read **"Out Of Me Went 43 Demons,"** written by (Evangelist) Antoinette Cannaday, published by Impact Christian Books, Inc. (ISBN # 0-89228-111-1) I was the one who successfully prayed for Evangelist Antoinette Cannaday and cast 43 demons out of her body. **Chapter 2** is a portion of her testimony and her deliverance after she received the baptism of the Holy Ghost.

PART II

TESTIMONIES AND

DELIVERANCE SESSIONS

Chapter 2

DELIVERANCE FROM 43 DEMONS
EVANGELIST ANTOINETTE CANNADAY

At the time of this writing, I have been delivered from 43 demons for over 16 years. I have been taught and trained in how to keep these demons out of my body. The word of God is my source. My teacher and exorcist is my pastor, Bishop Roy Bryant, Sr., D.D., Had it not been for him this testimony would not have been possible.

In January of 1980, I came to The Bible Church of Christ, Inc. located at 100 West 2nd Street, Mount Vernon, New York in the worse shape possible. I was suicidal and mentally depressed. The psychiatrist diagnosed me with a "chemical imbalance." I was medicated with 25 mg. Of Elavil to start, which soon increased to 150 mg. a day. Elavil, a mood-altering drug and antidepressant would also act as a nighttime sedative for me, considering the fact that I also suffered with insomnia. Although I was extremely tired during the day, which the psychiatrist said was a symptom of depression, I had a hard time falling asleep at night. Elavil would also act as an appetite booster, since I had no desire to eat. This too, as the psychiatrist said, was another symptom of depression. After, I regained my appetite, it would be possible for me to gain back the 40 lbs I had lost. Loss of weight, as my psychiatrist said, was another symptom of depression. I had a lot of symptoms but no answers as to why. My psychiatrists were at a loss for words. Their only answer was for me to keep taking my medication. The doctor said mental depression with suicidal tendencies could have been inherited or may have been brought on by an illness of some sort.

I really did not want to die, although I found myself sitting on a window ledge ready to jump. However, there was something, or someone, bigger than I, who was influencing my thoughts and my desires. They had become my personality. Whatever, these desires said to do, I did and the results were not always good. As a matter of fact abnormal behavior thoughts and desires were taking me down the road of self-destruction. I felt it would only be just a matter of time and my life would be over.

The ending of life did not only mean death at my own hands, but possible a long drawn out death sentence in a prison institution somewhere. Seemly, a deep rooted anger and a desire to kill had already sentenced me. I could never make anyone understand why I was so angry, not even my psychiatrist.

The day I stood before the judge, after spending a night in jail, I even left the judge in a puzzled state. He felt women like me should not be in prison. I could understand his bewilderment, because he was now looking at the real me. I was quiet, shy and scared. I was nothing like the young lady who had just inflicted my neighbor with bodily injury after beating her with a stick until I was exhausted and she lay unconscious. Anger erupted and I was left holding the bag. Thank God she did not die and she did not press charges against me. My neighbor was not hurt as bad as I thought. I really was sorry I got so angry, but I just could not help it. Someone greater than the circumstances that I was in was on my side because the judge was smiling, when he told me to go home and be a use to society.

Life after my short stay in prison continued to be a

40

bundle of troubled emotions and more personalities than I could count. I was full of pride one day; and unclean the next. I was stupid, lazy, tired, depressed, withdrawn,and with many lustful desires. I suffered with low self esteem, insecurity self-devaluation, rejection and self-destruction, just to name a few. I could not stand to look at myself unless I was fully painted up. For some unknown reason I had to hide the real me, because "she" was dirty ugly and insecure. I could only get rid of the insecure, dirty and ugly feelings when I painted my face and dressed in revealing outfits. I enhanced it by overmedicating myself. The pills made me forget and I could be anybody I wanted to be. They helped me to escape reality and enabled me to live in a world of fantasy. Soon I became a legalized junkie hooked on medications such as Percodans, Darvons, Librium, Tranzenes, Fiornial, Valiums and more.

January 1980, I walked into The Bible Church of Christ, Mt. Vernon, N.Y., not knowing that God was going to do a work in my life beyond human understanding. I recall the very first Sunday that I attended the service. Bishop Roy Bryant, Sr., Pastor was preaching the gospel. The word of God was soothing to my spirit. It was that which won me over. For the next four weeks I attended The Bible Church of Christ faithfully. I enjoyed the word and I anxiously waited for the confirmation of the word. It came through these words "It is prayer time in The Bible Church of Christ." Although I had been raised in a holiness church, I had never witnessed such an anointed prayer line as this. People were slain in the spirit right in front of my eyes. Others received miraculous healings, such as the lady who came in with mechanical aids to assist her with walking. When Bishop Bryant laid hands on her and called for healing to come forth, she began to run around the church.

41

Eyeglasses were taken off by different individuals and later hung in the pulpit to the glory of God. Some discovered that there was no longer a need for their medication and brought it back to the church where it joined all the other paraphernalia symbolizing that healing had taken place. These people **knew** they were healed and they rejoiced in it. I was sort of afraid to get on the prayer line right away because I had never witnessed the power of God on this level. I do remember Bishop Bryant, Sr., saying that God was manifesting Himself on the prayer line.

Four weeks later, when Bishop Bryant said, **"it is prayer time in The Bible Church of Christ,** I got on the prayer line to receive the baptism of the Holy Ghost. I did not quite know what to expect because I had been raised believing that we had to tarry for the Holy Ghost until we came through (manifestation of tongues) because Jesus told his disciples to "tarry" in the city of Jerusalem until they be endued with power from on high. However, I now understood that the Holy Ghost was already here and I did not have to "tarry," which actually means to wait. I could receive the Holy Ghost right now through the gift of laying-on-of-hands, exercised by Bishop Bryant, Sr., and all of his ministers.

I got on the prayer line and I remember thinking that Bishop Bryant, Sr., had a incredible amount of faith. He knew I would receive the Holy Spirit before he even layed hands on me. As a matter of fact, he told me so. He made me feel relaxed when he told me what to expect. He said, "Just thank **JESUS**, Sis," and I did. My "Thank you, Jesus" turned into the heavenly language, known as tongues according to Acts 2:4. Hallelujah! I received the Holy Ghost almost in less time than it took for me to walk down to the prayer line. Bishop Bryant called it the Holy Ghost line because others received that day just as I did. What a marvelous work in the name of Jesus.

Needless to say, I felt so good, I went home and I told all my relatives and even some of my neighbors. I also noticed that I had a peace that surpassed all understanding. At the very moment, I decided to trust Jesus with my mind. I took all of my medication and flushed it down the toilet. I also took all of my old indecent wardrobe and got rid of it. That included the pants, halters, shorts, makeup and all. I no longer desired to look like a half-dressed **Jezebel** and there was no need to hide the real me from the world. After all, I was a new creature in Christ Jesus. The Bible said so.

On Saturday, March 3, 1980 at 8:00 p.m. at The Bible Church of Christ, Mt. Vernon, New York, is a evening which will be etched in my mind forever. Almost three weeks after I received the baptism of the Holy Spirit, I entered into a mass demonology/deliverance service as a skeptic. I did not know what to expect or what to do regarding deliverance. The sanctuary was crowded; at least 500 people were there. I looked around to see if I could spot any demons. I had heard that the demons would be inside of the people and they would be cast out during the service. I wondered if any of these people had demons. They all looked normal to me.

That night the church held an element of reverence that created an expectation of joy among the people. The anointing of the Holy Ghost was so great that it vibrated like electricity throughout the entire church, One couldn't help but praise the true and living God, who was in the midst to bless His people. After the praise, prayer and singing, our pastor, Bishop Roy Bryant, Sr., stood to teach, aglow with the Holy Ghost anointing.

He explained that the teaching would be necessarily

long, but through it demons would be exposed. Bishop Bryant's teaching included **schizophrenia, depression, suicide**, and what psychiatry called **phobias, fears, abnormal behavior** patterns and **personalities**. Bishop Bryant identified them as demons, and I believed him. During the teaching I made up my mind that I would get rid of **depression** that night. I was not sure of the procedure, but I followed Bishop Bryant's instructions. When the teaching was concluded, Bishop Bryant announced he would pray the deliverance prayer.

We all stood and lifted our hands to Jesus, Not only did we pray, but under Bishop Bryant's leading, we renounced the Spirits by name, saying aloud that we no longer wanted them in our bodies. This disallowed their claims on us. I did as I was told.

With determination, I loudly said, **"Mental Depression,"** I don't want you anymore! I hate you! I want you out of my body and my mind! My mind belongs to Jesus." And I meant every word.

Still, I did not know what to expect. But being obedient to the instructions paid off for me in the service. Bishop Bryant had already explained how he would call them out by the spoken word after we had renounced them. The demons would have to leave under the authority of Jesus Christ.

As Bishop Bryant began to call out innumerable spirits, I stayed in a prayerful mood, but I could not help but watch what was happening around me. No one was talking or laughing. Demons began to cry out of people in loud voices. Some demons caused the people to cover their ears in order not to hear, but they heard anyway.

In the name of Jesus, demons were being cast out in the name of Jesus and people were rejoicing in their freedom.

When Bishop Bryant called mental depression, I felt a pull in my body the same time I heard a moan from my mouth. I thought it was just me, and I desired to remain quiet, not disturbing the service. But the moan became louder, and I clapped my hands over my mouth. My body began to rock back and forth. I had no control over what was happening to me. Bishop Bryant began to talk about the minds of God's people and he commanded the demons to come out of our minds. The demons could not stand the commands any longer. I saw my behavior patterns change immediately as I let loose a high-pitched wail. It was the demon of depression. Over and over again he screamed. Although the demon of depression was being tormented and made to leave his home (my body), I felt an inner peace that only the Holy Ghost can give. I felt no fear.

Soon one of the workers in the deliverance service came over to me. Softly she began to speak the word of God in my ear and she told me to release the mucus in my throat. I coughed and a blob of mucus came forth into the papers provided for us. At that very moment something happened. The torment was gone. The depressed state of mind left, and it was replaced with a feeling of peace and comfort. I was free at last. I felt that I could say with honesty that I was finally clothed in my right mind. Immediately, I began to praise God and cry. The years of torment from mental depression was finally over. Jesus did not let me down. The ministering I received in the deliverance service proved psychiatry to be a lie. I could not help but remember that the psychiatrist said that depression was hereditary, a chemical imbalance in the brain, that I would have to take Elavil the rest of my life. However, God's word says:

Phillipians 2:5:
Let this mind be in you, which was also in Christ Jesus:

Jesus Christ's mind is not depressed. Since 1980, I have had no need to take anti-depressants of any kind and I have not heard from mental depression.[3]

Amen.

---

[3]This excerpt of testimony was taken from *Out of Me Went 43 Demons*, chapter 10, page 110. Author, Evangelist Antoinette Cannaday

Chapter 3

THE ROOT OF MENTAL DEPRESSION
by the author

You have just read the testimony of Evangelist Antoinette Cannaday and her deliverance from the spirit of **Mental Depression**.

In my first book, *Manual On Demonology, Diary of An Exorcist,* (**Chapter 2, Page 47;) the section on depression**) I made this statement: *Mental Depression is the main area on which psychiatrists center their attention. Yet they do not understand the fullness of depression, anymore than we can understand death, until it comes to us. Death is a great mystery. How can the Lord say, "We shall live again?"*

Why can't the psychiatrist(s) understand depression? Because it is demonic. ***Depression*** *has many faces and many causes.* ***As an exorcist,*** *I not only look at the demon(s) of* ***depression****, but I ask, "How did he come in? Where was the violation?" I can name about twenty different ways. I not only deal with the present state, but the root cause. Not only do I look at* ***depression****, I search for the cause.*

This was the case with Evangelist Antoinette Cannaday. Her root was child molestation at the age of twelve. To further your knowledge and for you to understand the causes of her problems and others like her, I have placed in this book (next chapter) one of Evangelist Cannaday's private deliverance sessions.

Chapter 4

DEMONS SPEAKING #2 - DELIVERANCE SESSION

At the very beginning of this deliverance session, the demon Memory Recall took Evangelist Cannaday back to the age of twelve and threatened not to let her return. Let us begin there.

THE TWELVE YEAR OLD CHILD

"I want to be the apple in the top of the tree, Daddy. This man has dragged me all the way to the bottom. I hate him! I hate him! Look what he's doing to me. Daddy! Please don't let him. Please help me, Daddy. Where are you? I've got to wash; I can't tell Daddy I'm dirty, but it won't come off. I can't get clean. I am not your little girl anymore, Daddy. Don't let them get me. They're evil and they're dark. They're nasty! They want to take me out of the church, but I want to write, I am still going to write for Jesus. I can hear the words in my mind. They are in my head. I gave my Jesus my heart. I don't want to do these things. Their nastiness is creeping up on my body. Stop these things from using me, Please don't punish me, Daddy. It's not me; she's having sex. Don't punish me, I can't help it. Please, Daddy!

The demons were stirred up and angry. They said, "I, Roy Bryant, must pay for taking away a prize possession." Profanity came forth first and then abuse and threats as I layed my hands upon her for deliverance.

Demon

"Get your hands off me! She won't do nothing! She won't obey! It's your fault, Roy Bryant! She's ours! You have stepped on the wrong territory this time! You have really made a mistake! I am going to scandalize your name. You won't be able to hold your head up in this place!"

(Quickly the demon withdrew himself. She went from age 12 to 15 as different personalities/demons emerged and painful memories surfaced).

AGE 15

I'm going to have a baby. I'm too young. Daddy talk to me. It's her fault. She said I was ugly. She told me to paint myself. She said I would be clean. She dresses me up. Please believe me, Daddy"

I addressed the demons that spoke from her childhood. When I called out **Childhood Rape**, the demon became extremely angry, From the anger emerged another spirit.

Using discernment of the Holy Spirit, I then identified **Self-destruction, Self-Rejection, Self-devaluation, Hatred for Men** and **Suicide**. (When I identified these demons, it taught Evangelist Cannaday why she had placed very little value on herself and why she was on the road to self-destruction).

Demon

You are going to need a miracle to get us out of her.

Bishop Bryant, Sr.

I do have a miracle and His name is Jesus. (I then began to pray in tongues in the spirit. Other spirits began to come

out of her body. Next **Corrupt Communication** came
forth to speak:

Corrupt Communication

*"Give up the demonology ministry! Too many people
are hearing. Let it go. She won't work for my master. He
said to destroy her. She is now going to talk my language.
You are in enough trouble with my master. The radio isn't
enough, now it's television. How far do you think you are
going with this ministry, Roy Bryant."*

I then placed my hands on her and said to the demon
"Our God is a consuming fire" and I am going to burn you.
The Holy Ghost anointing has given me power and the
authority to burn the demons until they cried out.

Demon

*"You are destroying our psychiatry business. They
(the mentally ill) are ours. People come in here and they
listen to these testimonies. Because of you and this
deliverance ministry they are watching and believing.
They are beginning to believe that there is hope for the
mind. You are coming against our kingdom. The
psychiatrists are ours! We know they accomplish nothing,
but the people don't know it. You are supposed to be
scared. We keep coming against you, and you won't stop.
She's just like you; she won't stop. She's helping you, Roy.
We've got to stop you. (Changing the subject the demon
cried out) I am hungry! Get me some food! We like to eat.
We have desires just like you do. We have likes and
dislikes. We like to talk, that is why we go to the
psychiatrists, the stupid fools. We talk all the time, but we
want to hear someone talk to us. That is why we send the
patients to the psychiatrists. They talk back to us. They*

51

think they are talking to the patients. Then we get angry and go berserk. The psychiatrists thinks it the patients."

Realizing that the demons were telling on themselves, I let them speak to educate the people. I then quickly reminded the demons why they were now here in The Bible Church of Christ. "We cast out evil spirits." This only made the demons scream louder.

Demon

(Angrily) *"It's us! It's us! You don't have to drive us out. Just leave us alone."*

I identified the **Lying** demon and commanded that he come out of her body in the name of Jesus and the demon did. (Evangelist Cannaday later said that she began to have hope and encouragement when she found out that the demons had been lying to her all along.) Other demons began to speak again.

Demons

*"You are messing up our work, Roy Bryant! Why did you do that? You've done too much. You made **Jezebel** beg. You made **Pride** humble himself.* (this session is recorded on Demons speaking tape #1 where I cast out **Jezebel, Pride** and **Cursing** Demons. When I cast out the demon of **Pride,** the demon of **Jezebel** began to cry,. as she said, "Roy Bryant you got rid of my brother, **Pride. Jezebel** said, he was her brother.) I allowed the demons to continue to speak.

Demon

"Your head is as hard as rock. You won't believe anything. That's why you don't have any friends in the ministry. You won't give up and you won't shut up."

Bishop Bryant

My friend is Jesus. (I then began to burn these demons. They began to plead with me to compromise because they knew that their time was short.)

Demon

(The demons hated to hear that my friend was Jesus) *"Don't tell me that! I don't want to hear that! You need friends in the ministry to back you up. They say that this is a demon church. Do you know how many ministers are compromising with us, but you won't compromise. Your church could be filled with people, Roy, if you would just compromise. Leave us alone and we will set you up pretty.* [I then began to cite to the demons the word of God where Jsus was offered the kingdom of this world.]

Bishop Bryant
St. Matthew 4:5-10

Again, the devil taketh him [Jesus] up into an exceeding high mountain, and sheweth him all the kingdoms of the world and he the glory of them; And saith unto him, All these things will I give thee, if thou wilt fall down and worship me. Then saith Jesus unto him, Get thee hence, Satan: for it is written, Thou shalt worship the Lord thy God and him only shalt thou serve. The devil leaveth him, and behold, angels came and ministered unto him.

Demon

(The Liar demon cried out.) "I don't want to hear that. You need carpet, Roy, in Monticello, and Mount Vernon (two church sites). *We can give you gold and carpeting; we'll set you up. Teach the people about the Holy Ghost, fine. Just leave deliverance alone. We see the people*

coming. You are not supposed to have anyone on your side Satan told us to take all your people, all the people who love you. He said to go through the ministry and destroy the children.

I informed the demons that I was only allowing them to talk at such length because everything was being recorded.

Bishop Bryant
In the name of Jesus, see the cross and the blood.

Demon
I hate the cross. I hate the blood......I hate it.

Bishop Bryant
(I again began to quote the word found in found **St. John 14:12**) *"He that believeth on me, the works that I do shall he do also; and greater works than these shall he do; because I go unto the father."*

Demon
(Angrily) *"That's what's wrong with this church, too much Word! I hate the Word. Why don't you go into politics?"*

Bishop Bryant
You are our politics.

Demon
But I have to sit and listen to the word of God over and over again, the demon whined. It cuts me and torments me. (Bishop Bryant invited the demon to leave, but he protested that he had to stay). We've got to give you credit, Roy, you can really preach the Word, but people don't listen. It goes in one ear and out the other. We are doing a booming

business, because of the people's disobedience. Saints don't listen, they are hard-headed. When they disobey, we step in. Churches are full of hard-headed people. Young people don't obey their parents; we are taking the young people out one by one. Kids talk back. They are smoking and having sex. They do exactly what they want to do, but they are turning their backs on pastors and Sunday School teachers. Why do you think there are problems in the churches? We hear you talking to them. While you are talking, we are talking. They think we are their own thoughts. We are taking them out of the churches. These little brats don't want to obey. We hate them. The youth are going to die. We have to kill off the youth. We are going to keep them from the deliverance ministry. Then we'll attack the strong saints This is war!!!

During all the threats, I continued to pray. I allowed the demons to speak because this was being recorded in order to reveal their perverseness, hatred for mankind, and their plans.

Bishop Bryant

The blood of Jesus. Look at the cross of Calvary. In the name of Jesus. (I pounded into the demons verbally.) Evangelist Cannaday began to cough, and she continued to get deliverance. **Self-destruction, Self-rejection, Self devaluation, Memory recall, Hatred For Men, Corrupt Communication, Slumber, Tiredness** and others began to cry out in loud voices. I told her and the demons that she was clean through the word of God which he had spoken. **(St. John 15:3)** All of sudden we heard the most pitiful wail coming from a demon. It was the demon of **Uncleanliness.** He was very angry because I had informed Evangelist Cannaday of the truth. For 22 years, Evangelist

Cannaday said, she believed that she was unclean.

Uncleanliness

"Why did you tell her that? Now she knows the truth. (a hideous scream again came forth and a plea for mercy.) *Satan! Master! Please, Satan, where are you? Don't leave me, Master. Come help me! Where is my master? I am going to tell Satan on you, Roy Bryant. I am going to tell what you are doing to me. I have been in here so long. All these years she has been mine. Help me, Satan!*

Evangelist Cannaday began to cough violently as the demons one after another were expelled from her body. She then began to praise God. After 22 years of believing she was unclean, restoration began immediately following this powerful deliverance. That day Evangelist Cannaday was delivered from **Self-Devaluation, Self-destruction, Self-Destruction, Hatred for Men, Slumber, Tiredness, False Marriage, Uncleanliness and Corrupt Communication,** an overall total of 43 demons.[4]

---

[4] You may read more about the testimony of Evangelist Cannaday in her book, *Out of Me Went 43 Demons.* You may also listen to her deliverance on a three audio tape series. **"Demons Speaking #1, #2, #3** conducted by Bishop Roy Bryant, Sr. DD

Chapter 5

DEMONS SPEAKING #4 - DELIVERANCE SESSION

From *the Diary of an Exorcist*

This is a private deliverance session. I have placed this session in this book as well as in my first manual to let you see the nature of these demons.

Demon:

We're are going to close your church. We hate this church.

Bishop

Why do you hate this church?

Demon:

Because it is a holy. It is a holy church. We are going to destroy it. All your people are leaving.

Bishop:

That is because God is cleaning out the church

Demon:

It is going to be real clean. It is going to be empty. We took _____ (the demon named a very prominent person in this ministry)...Ha, Ha, Ha. That hurts doesn't it. It really hurts.

Bishop:

No, It doesn't hurt. God gave me peace about it. But the minister said that God took him out.

Demon:

He's being fooled. It was us. There will be no deliverance in his church and no woman preachers. We are going to have a ball in his church, and your people are going to follow him.

Bishop:

Who else did you take out of here? (the demons named others) What is your name?

Demon:

I am the father of lies. I lied to your people and they believed. We are going to take all the weak ones out of here. We are going to close this place.

Bishop:

How did you get them to leave?

Demon:

Embarrassment. You embarrassed them by telling them the truth. They don't believe in demons. Nobody believes that stuff but you. We even took your piano player.

Bishop:

My piano player? Who are you talking about? (I named one of our best musicians.)

Demon:

No, not him. (He then named someone else)

Bishop:

How did you take him?

Demon:

Money, filthy lucre. Ha! Ha! He wanted money. We

58

got money. This is war! We are going after the very elect and that means you.

Bishop:
Tell me, can a Christian have a demon?

Demon:
Of cause they can. You know that. Why ask me stupid questions.

Bishop:
Where do the demons work?

Demon:
In the flesh, the minds and the hearts. There are trillions of us; enough for all people. We want to be people, so we work in people.

Bishop:
What about the Holy Ghost? Where is the Holy Ghost?

Demon:
He is in the belly; in the bottom of the belly. We can't get there.

Bishop:
So you are telling me that a person who has the Holy Ghost can have demons.

Demon:
I just told you that. Yes, a Holy Ghost person can have a demon. Don't ask me any more stupid questions. Your God is a liar. He does not heal. If he healed why ain't _____ healed. We gave him cancer. We like to see people hurt and in pain. We like to see them suffer.

Bishop:

You cause cancer and afflictions?

Demon:

Yeah you know that. We are destroying the world with aids crack, drugs, cancer, prostitution, We are in control of the Mafia.

Bishop:

I know all of that. Why are you lying on me?

Demon:

To shut you up. I lied on you and on _____ (he named others). I told people on you. I am jealous. I am making division in the church. I spread gossip and lies. I have the power to scandalize. Now give up demonology!

Bishop:

You are a liar and you are jealous of God's people. You are an accuser of the brethren.

Demon:

I have been in this body since _____ was three years old. This is my home. I am suppose to stay in this body to destroy it. Now get your hands off of me, PLEASE! Your hands are hot! You are making me weak. You are burning me!

Bishop:

That is the anointing.

Demon:

Stop it! I don't like the anointing! I'll give you money, woman, gold, even the world. Just stop this demonology ministry. You are destroying our kingdom. You are tearing our kingdom down.

Evangelist Cannaday: (working along with me)
I've heard this before. You offered Jesus the kingdoms of this world if he would bow down and worship you. Remember the tape Demons Speaking #2, when you offered Bishop Bryant, Sr., money, new carpeting, for our Mt. Vernon church. You offered him gold, and women, if he would just stop working in demonology. He didn't stop and here I am.

Demon:
You and Evangelist Cannaday. We are going to destroy the both of you.

Bishop:
How are you going to destroy Evangelist Cannaday?

Demon:
We are going to take her mind. All of your ministers don't work in demonology. Ha! Ha! We even have some of them.

Bishop:
How do you have them? By what methods?

Demon:
Unbelief and lust. Some right in your churches don't believe and they are lusting. Preachers lust also. Men lust after other women and the women are lusting.

Bishop:
Spirit of Fornication come out of her!

Demon:

No, I am not! I have been here too long. I can't come out. She can't live holy.

Evangelist:

Oh yes she can, once we get rid of you.

Demon:

Oh there she goes. Shut Up! We are going to destroy you, Roy, and this church. You are being sued. Ha! Ha! We are going to take all your money. You know Jamaicans love money and you ain't seen nothing yet. We got another surprise in store for you.

Bishop:

What surprise? Who is this woman? She didn't really fall did she?

Demon:

None of your business. You are just being nosey and ye, she fell. Somebody in this church knows that lady but so what, we are going to take tithes and the offerings. You ain't going to have nothing.

Bishop:

You are a liar. The tithes and the offerings belong to God and the church has already prayed. The Bible says the gates of hell shall not prevail against the church.

Demon:

Oh shut up! I know the word better than you do. I was in heaven, remember. I wanted to be God. I am god now and I am the prince and the power of the air. I am god of this world and I work in churches. I get in the people and they do what I tell them to do. I work in the eyes and the body. I cause them to commit fornication, to gossip, to lie and to backbite. It is going to be hot in hell. A lot of people are going with me. I am taking all that I can. Saints are fornicating. We caused David to sin with Bathsheba. Look what we did. We caused him to lust after someone else's wife. What about Adam and Eve in the garden. We got power.

Bishop:
We are going to let you talk that we may educate the people.

Demon:
So, what? Some preachers are going to hell. Do you know that, Roy? Preachers don't believe you. Your own ministers don't believe you. They don't work in demonology. Your ministers are leaving.

Bishop:
Oh we've got many that believe. Some are working. Look at Evangelist Cannaday. She was delivered of 43 demons and she tells it. How long have you been in this body.

Demon:
I've been in her since _____ was 4 years old and I am not going to be delivered.

Bishop:
You said 3 years old before.

Demon:
So I lied. I've been here since _____ started going to foster homes. _____'s mother didn't want her.

Bishop:
If you know that how old is Sister _____ now ?

Demon:
31. (The demon was right.)

Bishop:
Now Sister _____ is going to get rid of you and is going to tell this testimony.

Demon:
Leave me alone! Get your hands off of me! You've already gotten rid of my brother. You've done enough. I hate you, Roy Bryant.

Bishop:
Hatred for Pastor, come out of her.

Demon:
Yeah, I am in here and I hate you. I hate leaders. I am going to destroy your name. We demons stick together. Your people don't stick together. If you get this division out, ____will destroy our kingdom. _____ is going to tell this.[5]

---

[5]   At the conclusion of this deliverance session, the individual began to praise God for the deliverance. Much deliverance was received on that day.

Chapter 6

DEMONS MOTIVATE THE WIFE OF A MINISTER

From the words of Bishop Bryant, Sr., DD
I have placed this testimony in this book as I have in Manual On Demonology (#1), Diary of An Exorcist, because this book titled "Satan, the Motivator," will show you just how Satan motivates whomsoever he will. He is thief that has come to steal, kill and destroy. His aim was to destroy this minister's wife, their marriage and reap havoc in the entire family. The following is her testimony in her words.

There was a time in my life that I felt all alone, in a terrible state of confusion and I had, or so I thought, no one to talk to. I am a minister's wife. Many people just assume that if you are a minister's wife, you don't have any problems. This could not be further from the truth. At times, we can feel as if everyone and everything else matters except for us.

I know now that my husband loves me; he is a good provider, he does what is best for our family and most importantly, he is a very good minister of the gospel. However, Satan blinded me to many of his good qualities. My problem surfaced at a time that my husband was saving money to buy us a home. I had credit cards and bills that he knew nothing about. I was on disability and my checks were not coming in regularly, therefore, I was falling behind in my bills. The pressure was on and every time my husband would refer to his bank account or his money, it would magnify in my mind "that is all he cares about is his money in his bank account!

The more I heard it the angrier I became. That money is more important to him than my problems. Why not steal it? Once the seed was planted to steal the money, I kept entertaining it. One day out of spite, I forged checks and began to steal the money. I kept pinching off of it until the entire $3,000 was spent. Once I fulfilled my desires, the Devil deserted me. My eyes were now open and I felt as if I was left holding the bag. I then realized by stealing the money, it was bringing poverty into my household. I tried to pay it back but I couldn't. I did this out of spite to hurt my husband and it backfired on me, because I was the one hurting. The Devil had tricked me. He made it look like I had did this on my own. Terrible thoughts began to manifest. Now my husband is not going to want me. He will probably want a divorce. Along with the thoughts, I acquired a terrible headache that I could not get rid of. My finances are twisted up and I am sinking deeper into quicksand with no way out. Maybe if I just take an overdose, I could just die quietly. Nobody would miss me.

When thoughts of **suicide** became the only way of this mess, It was then that I knew I needed deliverance. **Guilt** tried to stop me from calling Bishop Bryant, Sr., but I was desperate for deliverance. When I called him he told me that he knew something was wrong and he was waiting for my call. I began to confess all of my sins. I told Bishop Bryant, that this was not something that I would ordinarily do. Although I functioned, I felt as if I were two different people.

THE DELIVERANCE SESSION

While Bishop Bryant was working with me in deliverance, a spirit from childhood began to surface. The severity of the demons coming out of me caused my body to jerk. I felt like running as I tried to push Bishop Bryant away from me, but he continued to pray. The power of God working through Bishop Bryant, Sr., drove three spirits out of my body.

I looked up and saw the three spirits standing off in a corner and I was afraid they were going to come back into me, I screamed as Bishop Bryant comforted me by telling me they were outside of my body now and they could not come back. Although I saw the spirits, Bishop Bryant did not.

He asked me what they were doing. I told him they were looking at us and talking about him. They wanted to go out of the room, but they did not want to pass by him because they were afraid of him. We were situated near the door. As I was speaking, I saw them walking along the edge of the wall to go over to the other side of the room, but they could not get by Bishop Bryant, Sr. I screamed again for Bishop Bryant, not to let the Spirits get me. He again assured me that they couldn't. After I was fully assured and comforted, I began to smile and then laugh out loud. I noticed that immediately after the deliverance I felt burden free. The constant **headache** was gone and so were the depression and the desire to commit **suicide**.

Bishop Bryant then called my husband and explained to him my deliverance. He also cautioned him not to blame me for what the demons did. The family was thinking bad of me, but right now I need to be comforted and that none of the family should say anything to concerning this matter, although my father-in-law was very upset at the time because of the financial loss. My husband agreed with Bishop Bryant and he told him that he would make sure no one mentioned these things to me.

Today I thank God for Bishop Roy Bryant, Sr. Had he not prayed for me to get these demons out, no telling how far they would have driven me. I will always remember the Devil is no respecter of persons. He works on minister's wives as well as others. We are not exempt.

PART III

THE ORIGIN OF
SATAN, THE MOTIVATOR

Chapter 7

ONCE KNOWN AS LUCIFER

I am taking all Scriptures from the King James Version of the Bible. My aim is to give you the Word of God as it is written because Jesus said in:

St. John 5:39
Search the scriptures; for in them ye think ye have eternal life: and they are they which testify of me.

WHERE DID HE COME FROM?
While studying Satan, the Motivator, you will find that Satan has always caused trouble. Satan is a Hebrew word signifying adversary, enemy, an accuser. Most commonly known Satan is taken from Devil or Chief of the Evil Spirits. He is our opponent, meaning, as the Scriptures states, "adversary."

I Peter 5:8
Be sober, be vigilant; because your <u>adversary the devil</u>, as a roaring lion, walketh about, seeking whom he may devour.

Many people ask the question, "Where did Satan come from?" He came from heaven and the Bible proves it to be so.

In the book of Revelation the word of God tells us that there was war in heaven and Satan was cast out because he desired to take over heaven, but God moved against him to

71

cast him out. Let us search **Revelation** the **12**th chapter beginning at the **7**th verse.

A WAR IN HEAVEN

Revelation 12:7-10
And there was war in heaven: Michael and his angels fought against the dragon: and the dragon fought and his angels. And prevailed not: neither was their place found any more in heaven. And the great dragon was cast out, that old serpent called the Devil, and Satan, which deceiveth the whole world: he was cast out into the earth, and his angels were cast out with him. And I heard a loud voice saying in heaven, Now is come salvation, and strength, and the kingdom of our God and the power of his Christ: for the accuser of our brethren is cast down, which accused them before our God day and night.

This Scripture clearly answers the question where did Satan come from. Also we can look at:

THE FALL FROM HEAVEN

Isaiah 14:12-17.
How art thou fallen from heaven, O Lucifer, son of the morning! how art thou cut down to the ground, which didst weaken the nations! For thou hast said in thine heart, I will ascend into heaven, I will exalt my throne above the stars of God: I will sit also upon the mount of the congregation, in the sides of the north: I will ascend above the heights of the clouds; I will be like the most High. Yet thou shalt be brought down to hell, to the sides of the pit. They that see thee shall narrowly look upon thee, and

consider thee saying, Is this the man that made the earth to
tremble, that did shake kingdoms; That made the world a
a wilderness, and destroyed the cities thereof; that opened
not the house of his prisoners.

Also Jesus said, in the new testament:

St. Luke 10:18
I beheld Satan as lightning fall from heaven.

If we were to continue in Revelations we would see
where John the Revelator wrote:

Revelations 12:12:
Therefore rejoice ye heavens, and ye that dwell in them.
Woe to the inhabiters of the earth and of the Sea! for the
devil is come down unto you, having great wrath, [meaning
he came down angry because of his expulsion from heaven]
because he knoweth he hath but a short time.

SATAN, THE MOTIVATOR - GOD'S CREATION

This Biblical proof of Satan will lead us back to
Genesis, the book of beginning: Let us go to **Genesis
2:23-25.** I want us to see the creation after God made man
and watch Satan Motivating what God created:

And Adam said, this is now bone of my bones and flesh of
my flesh: she shall be called Woman, because she was
taken out of man. Therefore shall a man leave his father
and his mother, and shall cleave unto this wife; and they
shall be one flesh. And they were both naked, the man and
his wife, and were not ashamed.

In other words, man and woman were innocent; they both were naked and they were not ashamed to be so. This is what we call the dispensation of Innocent. However, that is another study. We are concentrating on Satan, The Motivator.

After Satan, God's created being, once known as Lucifer, was cast down from heaven, he started to work right away. Let us look at

SATAN IN THE GARDEN OF EDEN

Genesis 3:1.
Now the serpent was more subtil than any beast of the field which the Lord God had made. And he said unto the woman, Yea, hath God said, Ye shall not eat of every tree of the garden?

THE TEMPTATION
Let us stop here for a moment. This is what is known as the beginning of the temptation of Eve. God made man, placed him in a perfect environment and told him that he could eat of every tree of the Garden, except the tree that stood in the midst of the Garden, which was the tree of "Knowledge," to know good from evil. Although the tree of life was also in the Garden, God did not forbid them to eat of the tree of life.

Genesis 2:16-17
And the Lord God commanded the man, saying, Of every tree of the garden thou mayest freely eat: But of the tree of the knowledge of good and evil, thou shalt not eat of it: for in the day that thou eatest thereof thou shalt surely die.

But Satan, the motivator, working through the serpent said unto the woman in:

Genesis 3:4:
Ye shall not surely die.

Observe again what Satan says in:
Genesis 3:5:
For God doth know that in the day ye eat thereof, then your eyes shall be opened, and ye shall be as gods, knowing good and evil.

At this time, neither Eve or Adam had known evil. However, Satan is telling her that "in the day ye eat thereof, ye shall be as gods, (plural with a small "g") knowing good from evil." Let's read further:

Genesis 3:6-7
And when the woman saw that the tree was good for food, and that it was pleasant to the eyes, and a tree desired to make one wise, she took of the fruit thereof, and did eat; and gave also unto her husband with her; and he did eat. And the eyes of them both were opened, and they knew that they were naked; and they sewed fig leaves together, and made themselves aprons.

Now we see that their eyes were opened. This was the time of innocence and God had not revealed unto them "evil" or to know anymore than they did know. However, Satan presented this temptation to Eve, that she might be wise and be as gods knowing good from evil and that her eyes might be opened. This is the way Satan tempts. God does not tempt with evil; Satan does. Let us look at what James wrote to the church regarding temptation:

James 1:13-16

Let no man say when he is tempted, I am tempted of God: for God cannot be tempted with evil, neither tempteth he any man: But every man is tempted, when he is drawn away of his own lust, and enticed. Then when lust hath conceived, it bringeth forth sin: and sin, when it is finished, bringeth forth death. Do not err my beloved brethren.

Satan does not tell you the price that has to be paid for sin but he presents you with something that is attractive. The attraction to Eve was that her eyes would be open and she would be as a god, knowing good from evil. Believing that she would know as much as God knows, she did eat of the tree.

Chapter 8

THE FALL OF MAN AND
THE CURSES

We realize that Adam and Eve did sin and the results were that God cursed the earth, man, woman and the serpent.

THE SERPENT CURSED
To the serpent God said:
Genesis 3:14
Because thou hast done this, thou art cursed above all cattle, and above every beast of the field: upon thy belly shalt thou go, and dust shall thou eat all the days of thy life:

THE PROPHECY OF JESUS CHRIST:
Genesis 3:15
And I will put enmity between thee and the woman, and between thy seed and her seed; it shall bruise thy head, and thou shalt bruise his heel.

This is a prophecy speaking about the seed of the woman which is Jesus Christ. Virgin Mary is the only woman that had a seed. Every other woman that gave birth involved a man, except Christ. He was not born by the will of man.
St. John 1:13.
Which were born, not of blood, nor of the will of the flesh nor of the will of man, but of God.

77

Christ had no father on this earth. He is the only begotten son of God. It was the Holy Ghost that overshadowed Virgin Mary. When God cursed the serpent, he cast him down upon his belly, He told him that the seed of the woman was going to be his adversary. Christ and the Devil can never co-exist. It was God that put enmity between the seed of the woman and himself. This is why Jesus Christ said (at the temptation in the wilderness)

St. Luke 4:8
Get thee behind me, Satan; for it is written, Thou shalt worship the Lord thy God and him only shalt thou serve.

The head of the serpent is continually being bruised by the word of God, which is Jesus Christ. As the people of God, we have authority in the cross.

THE WOMAN CURSED
Unto Eve, God said:
Genesis 3:16
I will greatly multiply thy sorrow and thy conception; in sorrow thou shalt bring forth children; and thy desire shall be to thy husband, and he shall rule over thee.

THE GROUND CURSED
THE MAN CURSED
Unto Adam, God said:
Genesis 3:17-19
Because thou has hearkened unto the voice of thy wife, and hast eaten of the tree, of which I commanded thee, saying, Thou shalt not eat of it; cursed is the ground for thy sake; in sorrow shalt thou eat of it all the days of thy life; Thorns also and thistles shall it bring forth to thee; and thou shalt

eat the herb of the field; In the sweat of thy face shalt thou eat bread, till thou return unto the ground; for out of it wast thou taken; for dust thou art and unto dust shalt thou return.

We are not going to go into the all the curses, because that is a study by itself. The aim is to show you Satan, The Motivator. And how he motivated Eve to sin. According to the Scriptures, she gave unto her husband and he did sin also. The Word is telling us that Adam fell from the grace of God along with his wife and they were both driven out of the Garden of Eden. In the conclusion of the third chapter of Genesis we see where Adam and Eve were driven out of the garden.

Genesis 3:23-24
Therefore, the Lord sent him forth from the garden of Eden, to till the ground from whence he was taken. So he drove out the man; and he placed at the east of the garden of Eden Cherubims, and a flaming sword which turned every way, to keep the way of the tree of life.

God kept them away from the tree of life because the Bible tells us that if God left them in the Garden, they would have taken of the tree of life and lived forever; meaning man would never die.

Adam was the chief of sinners. He killed every man, woman, boy and girl upon the face of the earth. Apostle Paul verifies this when he said:

I Corinthians 15:21 & 22
For since by one man came death, ...
For as in Adam we all die

However, there is a doctrine stating that Adam was saved. There is no Bible to prove that Adam was saved; it is all based assumptions. Therefore, at this time we are going to another portion of this study to search the Scriptures to find whether Adam was saved Also, I am going to take you into a deeper study on the creation, the fall and the curses in the Garden of Eden, including **"The Curse of the Woman."** As I stated before, I will be repetitious, because this is a teaching manual. I ask you, **"Was Adam saved?"**

PART IV

SATAN MOTIVATES

THE GREAT

CONTROVERSY

Chapter 9

WAS ADAM SAVED?

There seems to be a great controversy by theologians, theological schools and the fundamentalists. You hear so many things over the airwaves because there are many types of teaching. I am really concerned and it has very much stirred me up. I am not going to tell anybody that I am infallible, but I do know my Bible and often I say to the people, if you make a statement and I can find in my Bible, the word that will contradict the statement you made and prove you wrong, then you are just wrong! The Bible does not contradict itself. Our lack of understanding causes the problem, God's word is Yea, yea; Nay, nay and Amen. The Lord spoke unto John The Revelator on the Island of Patmos these words:

Revelation 22:18-19
For I testify unto every man that heareth the words of the prophecy of this book, If any man shall add unto these things, God shall add unto him the plagues that are written in this book: And if any man shall take away from the words of the book of this prophecy, God shall take away his part out of the book of life, and out of the holy city, and from the things which are written in this book.

God is not threatening you, nor I, who hold onto the truth, but he is warning those who take His word and turn it around to suit themselves and do as he/she wills. In order for you to be free, you must know the truth. We cannot know and work in half truths because the whole truth is written in the word of God.

Let us go to Genesis, meaning the beginning; where Moses is the writer and let us hear the Lord speak to this man called Adam. We call him Adam because he was the first man. His name means "MAN." Every time God spoke to Ezekiel, he called him "son of man." What God was saying is, you are Adam, taken from the earth. Eve is woman because she was taken from the side of man.

We are now going to the Bible at the beginning of the creation of man and search and see if Adam was saved. Let us read:

Genesis 2:1-9.

Thus the heavens and the earth were finished, and all the host of them. And on the seventh day God ended his work which he had made; and he rested on the seventh day from all his work which he had made. And God blessed the seventh day, and sanctified it: because that in it he had rested from all his work which God created and made. These are the generations of the heavens and of the earth when they were created, in the day that the Lord God made the earth and the heavens, And every plant of the field before it was in the earth, and every herb of the field before it grew: for the Lord God had not caused it to rain upon the earth, and there was not a man to till the ground. But there went a mist from the earth, and watered the whole face of the ground. And the Lord God formed man of the dust of the ground, and breathed into his nostrils the breath of life; and man became a living soul. And the Lord God planted a garden eastward in Eden; and there he put the man whom he had formed. And out of the ground made the Lord God to grow every tree that is pleasant to the sight, and good for food; the tree of life also in the midst of the garden, and the tree of knowledge of good and evil.

The tree of life which Revelation speaks of is the same tree.

Revelations 22:1-2
And he shewed me a pure river of water of life, clear as crystal, proceeding out of the throne of God and of the Lamb. In the midst of the street of it, and on either side of the river, was there the tree of life, which bare twelve manner of fruits, and yielded her fruit every month: and the leaves of the tree were for the healing of the nations.

GOD'S COMMAND
Everything in the garden was good. Man could eat of every tree except the one tree. God did not say not to eat from the tree of life. He could have because man was created to live.

Genesis 2:16-17
And the Lord God commanded the man, saying, Of every tree of the garden thou mayest freely eat: But of the tree of knowledge of good and evil, thou shalt not eat of it: for in the day that thou eatest thereof thou shalt surely die.

That word surely brings me back to Nicodemus when God said unto him in:
St. John 3:7
Marvel not that I said unto thee, Ye must be born again...

"YE MUST" is a command. A command is something that is not altered. God did not say **maybe** to Adam. He

85

said "*surely.*" There is no question in my mind that God was not telling the truth. God did not ask a question. He made a positive statement. God cannot lie and He cannot fail.

Let us move ahead to:

Genesis 3:12
And the man said, the woman whom thou gavest to be with me, she gave me of the tree and I did eat.

Notice that Adam put the blame on the woman. However, God said "I commanded *you*." It was not a request. In the word of God, the commander-in-chief is God. He said, "Ye shall surely die," and they did exactly what God told them not to do.

ADAM-THE BRILLIANT MAN

I remember saying that Adam had no rights and some responded by saying that I should not use that terminology. I admit it was a very strong statement and the reason I made it was because God commanded Adam. Sometimes we think that Adam was just like you and I. Let me enlighten you. When God made Adam, there was not one blemish in his body. Adam had a mind second to no man that has ever been upon this earth. He was given the ability to name every fowl of the air and all the cattle that walked on this earth. Let us now go back to:

Genesis 2:19-20:
And out of the ground the Lord God formed every beast of the field, and every fowl of the air; and brought them unto Adam to see what he would call them: and whatsoever

Adam called every living creature, that was the name thereof. And Adam gave names to all cattle, and to the fowl of the air, and to every beast of the field;

Adam had some vocabulary. Every creeping thing, every fowl of the air, Adam named. It is stated that if an individual has a vocabulary of five-hundred words he is a genius. I tell you right now, to mention one-hundred words without stopping, without repeating and without hesitating would give anyone a tough time. Adam was a brilliant man. He named everything and he did not give anyone of God's creatures the same name. Therefore, when God told Adam he was going to die, Adam knew what God was talking about.

ADAM-THE MARRIED MAN
Genesis 2:24
Therefore shall a man leave his father and his mother, and shall cleave unto his wife: and they shall be one flesh.

Notice that the word says Adam and his wife. Another lie that is told is that Adam was not married. All these untruths are floating around and are in Christiandom today. God joined them together: They were joined together <u>as one in spirit</u>. God can unite together. When man and woman cohabitate, (through sexual intercourse) they become as one.

ADAM-THE INNOCENT MAN

Genesis 2:25
And they were both naked , the man and his wife and were not ashamed.

This is the first dispensation, Innocence. It is one of the seven dispensations that God employed in dealing with man. The reason I am bringing this out, is to show you that Adam and Eve were totally innocent. They were naked and did not know that they were naked.

I liken Adam and Eve to newborn babies. A baby can lay upon a table naked and a thousand people can be around him, and the baby will not care. He is just having a good time. The parents know that he is naked, but the baby is not aware of his nakedness. This is the state Adam and Eve were in, because God made them innocent.

THE CHALLENGE

Let us now refer to:

Genesis 3:1-5

Now the serpent was more subtil than any beast of the field which the Lord God had made. And he said unto the woman, Yea, hath God said, Ye shall not eat of every tree of the garden? And the woman said unto the serpent, We may eat of the fruit of the trees of the garden; But of the fruit of the tree which is in the midst of the garden, God hath said, Ye shall not eat of it, neither shall ye touch it, lest ye die. And the serpent said unto the woman, Ye shall not surely die: For God doth know that in the day ye eat thereof, then your eyes shall be opened, and ye shall be as gods, knowing good and evil.

Here we have a challenge. The Devil challenged God in heaven, and one third of the angels believed his lie. (Read **Revelations 12:1-12**) Satan is again challenging God. God had given to them the garden and He gave them His commandment. Satan, the adversary went against God. Remember this, the Devil cannot do, and will not do

88

anything right. He refuses to do so. No demon will do anything right or legal; if he does anything, it is illegal and against God's word. Demons will always work contrary and against God's word. If it is legal the Devil wants nothing to do with it because his aim is to destroy.

St. John 8:44

Ye are of your father the devil, and the lusts of your father ye will do. He was a murderer from the beginning, and abode not in the truth, because there is no truth in him. When he speaketh a lie, he speaketh of his own: for he is a liar, and the father of it.

The Devil got into the serpent in a very subtil way. He approached Eve, to beguile her. (Read **Genesis 3ʳᵈ** chapter) In other words just as the world says, men jive the women to get what they want. Therefore, we can say that Satan deceived Eve. He pretended that he was going to enlighten her and give her some truth. At the same time he was out to destroy her. It is a spirit of **"DECEPTION"** and he deceived Eve.

Genesis 3:5

For God doth know that in the day ye eat thereof, then your eyes shall be opened, and ye shall be as gods, knowing good and evil.

God did not intend for them to know good from evil at this particular time. That is why he forbid them to eat of that tree. People are always curious. The word of God in the book of James states:

James 1:13-14

Let no man say when he is tempted, I am tempted of God:

*for God cannot be tempted with evil, neither tempteth he
any man: (14) But every man is tempted, when he is drawn
away of his own lust, and enticed.*

Satan showed Eve the tree.
Genesis 3:6
*And when the woman saw that the tree was good for food,
and that it was pleasant to the eyes, and a tree to be
desired to make one wise,*

The Devil told her that. God did not give Eve that
knowledge
*she took of the fruit, thereof, and did eat and gave also unto
her husband with her; and he did eat.*

THE COVER-UP
After Adam and Eve sinned, there mind went directly
to their nakedness.
Genesis 3:7
*And the eyes of them both were opened, and they knew that
they were naked; and they sewed fig leaves together, and
made themselves aprons.*

Adam put fig leaves upon himself when he found out
that he was naked. This was his way of covering his
transgression. The Bible does not say that God covered or
blotted out Adam's transgression. But, Adam tried to cover
his transgressions.

HE THAT COVERS HIS SINS...
Proverbs 28:13
He that covereth his sins shall not prosper.

Genesis 3:8-13:

And they heard the voice of the Lord God walking in the garden in the cool of the day: and Adam and his wife hid themselves from the presence of the Lord God amongst the trees of the garden. And the Lord God called unto Adam and said unto him, Where art thou? And he said, I heard thy voice in the garden, and I was afraid, because I was naked; and I hid myself. And he said, Who told thee that thou was naked? Hast thou eaten of the tree, whereof I commanded thee that thou shouldest not eat? And the man said, The woman who thou gavest to be with me, she gave me of the tree, and I did eat. And the Lord God said unto the woman, What is this that thou has done? And the woman said, The serpent beguiled me and I did eat.

When God confronted them, Adam blamed the woman and the woman blamed the serpent. After Adam and Eve ate of the forbidden fruit and found themselves naked they took fig leaves and covered their naked bottom parts. From that time on we have had trouble with our bottom parts. The Devil started it and it is still a problem today.

Here again we must be very careful because there are teachers that will tell you that their sin (taking of the forbidden fruit) was a sexual act and the Devil fathered Cain. It is untrue and is not found in the Scriptures. Yet, you have people that are teaching this and it is widespread. Also, you hear other saying that God sacrificed an an animal to make coats of skins to clothe them. The Bible does not say that, therefore, we have got to watch out for man's mind. If God did not say it, leave it alone. If God says it, stand on it. He did not say apple, orange or what type of fruit it was, but I do know that it was fruit because God said it. It was not a sexual act. Man with his twisted mind is always coming up with something. We must always be able to counteract all these lies. These same people call themselves teachers of the word of God.

Genesis 3:14-16:

And the Lord God said unto the serpent, Because thou hast done this, thou art cursed above all the cattle, and above every beast of the field, upon thy belly shalt thy go and dust shalt thou eat all the days of thy life: And I will put enmity between thee and the woman, and between thy seed and her seed; it shall bruise thy head, and thou shalt bruise his heel. Unto the woman he said, I will greatly multiply thy sorrow and thy conception; in sorrow thou shalt bring forth children; and thy desire shall be to thy husband and he shall rule over thee.

As I stated in the previous chapter (The Fall of Man And The Curses), When God cursed the serpent, he cast him down upon his belly and he told him that the Seed of the woman, Jesus Christ, the Word of God, was going to be his adversary. Christ and the Devil can never co-exist.

God took the desire of the woman and gave it unto the man. He now would rule over her and from that time forth birth would come forth in sorrow. The woman would be saved in childbearing according to:

I Timothy 2:15:

Notwithstanding, she shall be saved in childbearing, if they continue in the faith and charity and holiness with sobriety.

(Read chapter 13 *"CURSE OF THE WOMAN"*)

Let me interject this: The Hebrew women, as recorded

in the book of Exodus, were not as the Egyptian Woman; they had easy birth and brought forth quickly. King Pharoah ordered that the male children be killed. He spoke this to the midwives:

Exodus 1:16.
And he said when ye do the office of a midwife to the Hebrew women, and see them upon the stools; if it be a son, then ye shall kill him; but if it be a daughter, then she shall live.

However the Hebrew women gave birth quickly. Read the response of the midwives:

Exodus 1:18-19
And the king of Egypt called for the midwives, and said unto them, Why have ye done this thing, and have saved the men children alive? And the midwives said unto Pharaoh, Because the Hebrew women are not as the Egyptian women; for they are lively, and are delivered ere (before) the midwives come in unto them.

The woman shall be saved in childbearing does not mean if the woman died in childbirth she would go to heaven, that is what the old women thought. It means she would be saved from the misery and the agony of giving birth.

Let us go to:

Genesis 3:17-19:
And unto Adam, he said, Because thou has hearken unto the voice of thy wife, and hast eaten of the tree, of which I commanded thee, saying, Thou shalt not eat of it: cursed is the ground for thy sake; in sorrow shalt thou eat of it all the days of thy life; Thorns also and thistles shall it bring

forth to thee: and thou shalt eat the herb of the field: In the sweat of thy face shalt thou eat bread, till thou return unto the ground: for out of it wast thou taken: for dust thou art, and unto dust shalt thou return.

God cursed the serpent, the woman, the man and the ground. In other words God said you are going to have hardships. The earth is saying, I am not going to yield myself to you. The farmer has a hard ground to hoe. We have so much misery in our bodies because God's whole creation is moaning, waiting for Christ to manifest himself. Then will man and the earth be delivered from this curse. God proves this in his word:

Romans 8:18-25

For I reckon that the sufferings of this present time are not worthy to be compared with the glory which shall be revealed in us. For the earnest expectation of the creature waiteth for the manifestation of the sons of God. For the creature was made subject to vanity, not willingly, but by reason of him who hath subjected the same in hope. Because the creature itself also shall be delivered from the bondage of corruption into the glorious liberty of the children of God. For we know that the whole creation groaneth and travaileth in pain until now. And not only they, but ourselves also, which have the firstfruits of the Spirit, even we ourselves groan within ourselves, waiting for the adoption to wit, the redemption of our body. For we are saved by hope: but hope that is seen is not hope: for what a man seeth, why doth he yet hope for? But if we hope for that we see not, then do we with patience wait for it.

ADAM THE UNSAVED MAN

There is no Bible to back up that Adam was saved. The one verse that they use to say that Adam was saved is:

Genesis 3:21:

Unto Adam also and to his wife did the Lord God make coats of skins, and clothed them.

Man is saying that this skin was a type of righteousness and a type of Christ. This is just assumption and you cannot go by assumption because anything that is contrary to the word of God is not truth.

Theologians and teachers said that God slew an animal and this is the blood sacrifice. The blood was shed for remission of Adam's sin. Why would God have to kill an animal to cover their nakedness. Where did God get Adam from? God got him from the dust of the earth. Could not God have gotten skins the same way that he made man. They still do not have any Bible to prove that God killed an animal and offered up a sacrifice to himself. Neither can anyone find in the Bible to justify that Adam was saved. God said *"for in the day that thou eatest thereof thou shalt surely die."* If God did cover their sins, then the Devil was right in the first place and God lied. The Devil said: "ye shall not surely die," and God said, *"you shall surely die."* This was a spiritual death. Physically Adam lived to be nine hundred and thirty years old and then he died.

Genesis 5:5

And all the days that Adam lived were nine hundred and thirty years: and he died.

The same people will agree to the fact that Adam and Eve died spiritually, but not physically. Well if you say they died spiritually, how are you going to say in the next breath that Adam was saved. Adam was a sinner of sinners. Adam killed every man, woman, boy and girl upon the face of the earth. Apostle Paul verifies this:

I Corinthians 15:22
For as in Adam we all die

Genesis 3:21 is what is used to say that Adam was saved. Just one verse taken out of context, yet, we have a whole Bible.

God has to cover our sins. How does he cover our sins? Our sins are covered by the blood of Jesus. That is the reason why the Scriptures say:

Colossians 2:14.
Blotting out the handwriting of ordinances that was against us, which was contrary to us, and took it out of the way, nailing it to his cross;

This is what Jesus did in his death. He was pierced in his side and out came blood and water. The blood represents the remission of sins:

Hebrews 9:22.
And almost all things are by the law purged with blood; and without the shedding of blood is no remission of sins

The water represents the Holy Spirit:

St. John 4:14.
But whosoever drinketh of the water that I shall give him shall never thirst; but the water that I shall give him shall be a well in him a well of water springing up into

everlasting life.

The death of Jesus blotted the transgression of the ordinances that was against us. The ordinances against us was Adam's transgression. Sin, after the similitude of Adam, came upon us all, even those that had not sinned. Again, I repeat, Adam brought death upon the whole world. Adam died an unsaved man.

BY ONE MAN DEATH - ANOTHER MAN LIFE

Romans 5:12-14
Wherefore, as by one man sin entered into the world, and death by sin; and so death passed upon all men; for that all have sinned; For until the law sin was in the world: but sin is not imputed when there is no law. Nevertheless death reigned from Adam to Moses, even over them that had not sinned after the similitude of Adam's transgression, who is the figure of him that was to come.

Adam was the figure of Jesus Christ to come. Sin and death came by one man. How can anyone tell me that God is going to save Adam, who brought sin on all mankind and all of us are held accountable for our sin. That does not even make sense. The Bible makes it plain that sin and death came upon us all. Death reigned from Adam to Moses unto the coming of the law on Mount Sinai. In other words, Death! Death! Death! Adam slew all of mankind; all generations. Even after the law, sin is charged unto us.

The reason sin was charged unto us is because God said, "thou shall not kill, thou shall not commit adultery," etc. However, we still do these things. Sin is the transgression of the law. Therefore, how can we say that Adam

97

was saved, when we have all this sin upon us because of Adam.

Again, I ask the question, "How can anyone say that Adam was saved?" I have given a lot of Bible proving that Adam died. I have no Bible telling me that Adam's sin was forgiven him. Adam died.

I Corinthians 15:20-22.

But now is Christ risen from the dead, and become the first fruits of them that slept. For since by man came death, by man came also the resurrection of the dead. For as in Adam all die, even so in Christ shall all be made alive.

Again, I repeat Adam means earth. Since man was taken from the earth, he is called Adam. God's word tells us that in Adam we all die and in Christ we are all made alive (*came the resurrection of the dead*). This is why Christ had to put on the humanity when he came. Jesus was called the son of David and the son of man. Jesus was his earthly name.

St. Matthew 1:21

Thou shalt call his name Jesus: for he shall save his people from their sins..

Christ became an Adam, however, he was a spiritual Adam. He is our high priest. Just as Adam killed us, spiritual Adam came that we might be able to approach him. Apostle Paul stated:

Hebrews 5:1-3

For every high priest taken from among men is ordained for men in things pertaining to God, that he may offer both gifts and sacrifices for sins. Who can have compassion on

98

the ignorant, and on them that are out of the way; for that he himself also is compassed with infirmity. And by reason hereof he ought, as for the people, so also for himself, to offer for sins.

The reason they are taken from among men is that they might minister the things of God to man and to make intercession for man on the behalf of man in the things pertaining to God. In other words God will never choose or do like mankind. For example, when an anti-poverty program is set, the choice for leadership is a rich man, someone born with a silver spoon in his mouth. You never see them appoint someone who is broke, down and out, and who knows and understands poverty. That is the individual they should get. Many of the men that have been appointed to head the farmer's program are men that have never farmed a day in their life. But they are set up for political reasons. God does not work that way, in other words, God wants (us) to rejoice in our labor because we are supposed to lay the fruit. We become the husbandman. Don't think that you are going to build on my foundation. It doesn't work that way. Any time you take a minister who raises up a work, (take me, for instance) and move him to another church it does not work. God always raises up somebody in the midst that has been a part of the work; that way God can work. He will not allow someone else to come in and rejoice over my labor. If He takes me out of the way, that is another story. He will then put somebody else in my place. A man can build up something and another will move him and put him someplace else. However, God does not work that way. He will make you prove yourself. He will make you sweat and labor. God will let you see that work grow right from the ground. When it grows from the ground up, then God will let you rejoice in your labor. God took David from following after the sheep. He could have taken someone highly esteemed in Israel, but he did not do it that way.

The summary of this is: Christ brought the resurrection unto us, but Adam killed every one of us. Thank God for the resurrection. The reason humanity is having a tough time is because of Adam. What we are required to do is preach the 2nd Adam to them. We let them know that the 1st Adam killed them, however there is another Adam. He is Jesus Christ our Lord.

Now if you find something where the Devil is right and God is wrong, show it to me, because the Devil was right and God was wrong if Adam lived. Just as Adam died spiritually, we can be walking dead. Just as Apostle Paul said:

Ephesians 2:1-5

And you hath he quickened, who were dead in trespasses and sins; Wherein in time past ye walked according to the course of this world, according to the prince of the power of the air, the spirit that now worketh in the children of disobedience; Among whom also we all had our conversation in times past in the lusts of our flesh, fulfilling the desires of the flesh and of the mind; and were by nature the children of wrath, even as others. But God, who is rich in mercy, for his great love wherewith he loved us, Even when we were dead in sins, hath quickened us together with Christ, (by grace ye are saved).

The Bible says that Jesus is going to come back and judge the quick and the dead. We are the quick, those that have received the baptism of the Holy Ghost. The dead are

100

those who have not received the Holy Ghost. It is God that will quicken our mortal bodies as it is stated in the book of Romans. We will also read the various Scriptures concerning what Apostle Paul had to say regarding the Holy Ghost.

Romans 8:11
But if the Spirit of him that raised up Jesus from the dead dwell in you, he that raised up Christ from the dead shall also quicken your mortal bodies by his Spirit that dwelleth in you.

Romans 8:9
...Now if any man have not the Spirit of Christ, he is none of his.

Hebrews 12:14
Follow peace with all men, and holiness, without which no man shall see the Lord.

I Corinthians 12:3
Wherefore I give you to understand, that no man speaking by the Spirit of God calleth Jesus accursed: and that no man can say that Jesus is the Lord, but by the Holy Ghost.

Let us read and understand what the Apostle Paul was saying in

I Timothy 2:13-14:
For Adam was first formed, then Eve. And Adam was not deceived, but the woman being deceived was in the transgression.

Adam was first formed. In the very beginning, sin started with Eve. She was first deceived by the Devil. When Eve brought the fruit to Adam, he went on and

101

obeyed his wife. Adam could have simply said this, "Forget about this thing. You know God told us not to eat of this tree. I remember one of the old saints told me that God had given her a revelation. Her revelation was: When Eve sinned and brought the fruit to Adam that Adam had to eat of it. Had he not eaten of it, he would have lost his helpmate. In other words, God told her he had to eat of the fruit in order to keep them both on the same level.

I said to her, I cannot see God giving you a revelation on that because our sins are personal. The Lord said:

Ezekiel 18:4
...The soul that sinneth, it shall die.

God made everyone of us individuals. Every word is to us as an individual. When we are put together, then we become cities, towns, countries. Even our salvation is an individual thing. The Lord says:

St. Matthew 11:28-30.
Come unto me, all ye that labor and are heavy laden, and I will give you rest. Take my yoke upon you, and learn of me; for I am meek and lowly in heart: and ye shall find rest unto your souls. For my yoke is easy and my burden is light.

This is an invitation that has been given unto us. Jesus said,

St. John 12:32.
And I, if I be lifted up from the earth, will draw all men unto me.

It is up to us to accept that invitation. No doubt many

people believe that Adam had to sin. In other words Adam without sin, would have remained in the garden and Eve would have been cast out. I don't know what God would have done for Adam and I am not going to try and say what God would have done because the Bible does not say anything like that. The fact is that there is no such thing as having to sin to stay on a level with your mate. I cannot buy that. When I said this the woman got angry with me; *"Well God revealed that unto me, were her words."* This woman had been carrying this lie all of these years and I know that it is a lie from the bottomless pit of hell. I do know if Adam had kept a perfect life and Eve had sinned, Eve would not have been his wife anymore.

However, Adam did sin. Not only spiritual death came by Adam, but natural death as well. Many of our bodies are afflicted because of the curse. Diseases and all of this came by the sins of Adam. This is why mankind is suffering. The Lord said:

St. John 10:10.
I am come that they might have life and that they might have it more abundantly.

Because of sin, many of us are dying before our time. The Bible says that it is promised to us threescore years and ten (70) and by reason of strength fourscore (80 years).

Psalms 90:10
The days of our years are threescore years and ten; and if by reason of strength they be fourscore years, yet is their strength labour and sorrow; for it is soon cut off, and we fly away.

103

In the beginning of our Bible men lived 900 years and more right on down to the time of the flood. The years decreased after the flood. Sin has taken its toll over the years and man's life span is being cut shorter and shorter. In some countries, such as America, humanity is living a little longer due to medical science. Yet, we still have people in countries where it is almost impossible to live past 25 to 40 years old. In many of our countries, if they live to be in that age range, that is living a long time. A large percentage of them die. Death is still coming by sin. When we receive the baptism of the Holy Spirit, some of the afflictions sin put upon us God took off of us. God extended our lives and gave us longevity. Remember these words:

Jude 14-21:

And Enoch also, the seventh from Adam prophesied of these, saying, Behold, the Lord cometh with ten thousands of his saints, To execute judgment upon all, and to convince all that are ungodly among them of all their ungodly deeds which they have ungodly committed, and of all their hard speeches which ungodly sinners have spoken against him. These are murmurers, complainers, walking after their own lusts; and their mouth speaketh great swelling words, having men's persons in admiration because of advantage. But beloved, remember ye the words which were spoken before of the apostles of our Lord Jesus Christ; How that they told you there should be mockers in the last time, who should walk after their own ungodly lust. These be they who separate themselves, sensual, having not the Spirit. But ye, beloved, building up yourselves on your most holy faith, praying in the Holy Ghost.

Just as Jude wrote to the church:

Jude 1:3

Beloved, when I gave all diligence to write unto you of the common salvation, it was needful for me to write unto you, and exhort you that ye should earnestly contend for the faith which was once delivered unto the saints.

PART V

SATAN MOTIVATES

HERESIES AND SCRUPLES

Chapter 10

CELIBACY OF THE
ROMAN CATHOLIC PRIEST:

It is bad to use one verse to explain your doctrine. It is Heresies. Here is a good example: A Chancellor of a Roman Catholic University made a statement that the Roman Catholics use one verse to explain their doctrine, the celibacy of the Priest. They are not allowed to marry and cohabitate because Jesus said:

St. Matthew 4:10
Get thee hence, Satan: for it is written, Thou shalt worship the Lord thy God, and him only shalt thy serve.

Again, I repeat this one verse is used for the celibacy of the Roman Catholic Priest. It is amazing how they think. Abraham had a wife, Issac had a wife, Jacob had a wife, Peter had a wife and Virgin Mary had a husband. Yet they say celibacy is the portion for the priest. See how people can take one verse and bring such disaster upon so many souls. That is heresy! All false doctrine starts with just one verse and a lie. That is just how the Devil works. It is heresy! Heresies are the most deadly thing on this earth. Do you know who bears heresies? A heretic!

THE HERETICS?
A heretic is one who brings false doctrine and God will slay a heretic. In the first church, God commanded that all heretics and sodomites be put out of the land. This same

God said to Adam *"ye shall surely die."* I say unto any man that says Adam was saved, *"Give me Bible to prove it."* The Bible says:

Romans 3:4.
...let God be true, but every man a liar; as it is written, That thou mightest be justified in thy sayings, and mightest overcome when thou art judged.

We must stand on God's word and let everything else be a lie. God does not care whether you are the pope, bishop, teacher, or theologian. Apostle Paul wrote to the church at Galatia:

Galatians 1:6-9
I marvel that ye are so soon removed from him that called you into the grace of Christ unto another gospel. Which is not another; but there be some that trouble you, and would pervert the gospel of Christ. But though we, or an angel from heaven, preach any other gospel unto you, let him be accursed. As we said before, so say I now again, If any man preach any other gospel unto you than that ye have received, let him be accursed.

If we fail or disbelieve one Scripture, we will disbelieve something else, because one Scripture ties itself into another. The Scriptures are interwoven. You cannot study and learn just one Scripture because that one portion will open up into another portion of Scripture. In other words it is impossible to really learn one verse without opening up another verse. The Bible is like a puzzle. If you miss putting one piece in place, you cannot finish that puzzle.

Chapter 11

HAD NOAH EVER SEEN RAIN?

Here is another lie. The lie that Noah had never seen rain. The Scripture that is used is this:

Genesis 2:5,6
...For the Lord God had not caused it to rain upon the earth, and there was not a man to till the ground. But there went up a mist from the earth, and watered the whole face of the ground..

Yes God did cause a mist to fall upon the ground. However, we have got to take into account the other part of that verse: *"and there was not a man to till the ground."* This was before the creation of Adam.

It is hard for us to take God at his word. They say that Noah had not seen rain. Another verse used for this is:

Hebrew 11:7:
By faith Noah, being warned of God of things not seen as yet, moved with fear, prepared an ark to the saving of his house; by the which he condemned the world, and became heir of the righteousness which is by faith.

"...being warned of God of things not seen as yet," The things, not as yet seen, were the destruction of the earth and a flood of this magnitude, so great that he would have to build an ark. One must remember that God did not create man or this earth for destruction. However because of the

111

state of mankind, God did just that. Let us read:

Genesis 6:5-7.

And God saw that the wickedness of man was great in the earth, and that every imagination of the thoughts of his heart was only evil continually. And it repented the Lord that he had made man on the earth, and it grieved him at his heart. And the Lord said, I will destroy man whom I have created from the face of the earth; both man, and beast, and the creeping thing, and the fowls of the air; for it repenteth me that I have made them.

The magnitude of the destruction which we have just read (verses 5-7) is what Noah had not as yet seen. This is what the writer of Hebrews was speaking about in the 11th chapter, which we know to be the chapter of faith. By faith Noah built the ark.

Again, I repeat it is hard for us to take God at his word. If we take the generations from Adam to Noah you will find that it was about the space of 1550 years. That is a lot of generations. If you count these generations even to Methuselah, who lived to be the oldest man on the face of the earth, you would have to ask yourself the question, how could this world exist without rain for 1550 years. If you tell a scientist that, they would laugh at you. If we had no rain for just a period of one year, I can tell you what would happen. We certainly cannot drink the salt water and the mist that come from the ground. There is no place in the Bible that says when God told Noah that it was going to rain, that Noah asked God, what is rain? The statement that Noah never saw rain is a lie that is taught and there is no have no Scripture to back it up. Again, I repeat, God sent a mist to water the ground because there was not a man to till

112

the ground. God was showing the process whereby the first earth yielding seed, God put it into the ground after its kind. When the mist watered the earth, it then began to bring forth every seed after its own kind. This is the first process whereby He caused the first seed to grow. God saw that everything was good. Man was the last thing God made on the sixth day. God put man in a perfect environment that was already set up. It is amazing how man thinks. Sometimes, I cry because my spirit becomes so grieved. The Bible is the only book on the face of God's earth that man will take out of context. Yet, if people are given a secular book, it will be kept in context. If they are given a telephone book, they will look at it in alphabetical order. They will not look for me, Bishop Bryant, under "Smith," but they will take the Bible and do just that. Do you know why? Because is diabolical. It is heresy and through the heretics Satan is out to discredit God's word.

Chapter 12

HAS GOD PROMISED
TO SAVE YOUR HOUSEHOLD?

Another doctrine is, the Lord promised to save you and your household. Apostle Paul was speaking directly to the Phillipian jailer who asked the question:

Acts 16:30-34
Sirs, what must I do to be saved? And they [Paul and Silas] *said Believe on the Lord Jesus Christ, and thou shalt be saved, and thy house. And they spake unto him the word of the Lord, and to all that were in his house. And he took them the same hour of the night, and washed their stripes; and was baptized, he and all his, straightway. And when he had brought them into his house, he set meat before them, and rejoiced, believing in God with all his house.*

The key is the Philippian jailer and his household believed. Remember Apostle Paul was speaking directly to the Philippian jailer with a believing household. Jesus said:

St. Matthew 10:34-38
Think not that I am come to send peace on the earth: I came not to send peace, but a sword. For I am come to set a man at variance against his father, and the daughter against her mother, and the daughter-in-law against her mother-in-law. And a man's foes shall be they of his own household. He that loveth his father or mother more than

115

me is not worthy of me; and he that loveth son or daughter more than me is not worthy of me.

Acts 2:39

Apostle Peter said:

For the promise is unto you, and to your children, and to all that are afar off, even as many as the Lord God shall call.

God made a promise to call many of us, but never promised to save our households. Amen.

PART VI

SATAN AND THE WOMAN

Chapter 13

THE CURSE OF THE WOMAN

Isaiah 4:1

And in that day seven women shall take hold of one man, saying, We will eat our own bread, and wear our own apparel: only let us be called by thy name, to take away our reproach.

The time is now for the above Scripture, because this is what is happening today. There is an increase in the women that are living with men and producing one baby after another. The one thing that they are concerned about is the name. These women may not want to marry him, however, on the birth certificate, they will have the man's name. A child born out of wedlock, according to the word of God is a "bastard." (Read Deuteronomy 23:2.) Therefore, if they use the man's name they are declaring that their child is legitimate.

It is amazing. We don't know who is legally married today; we just take it for granted. Many couples have come into The Bible Church of Christ, Inc. and they were married after they came into the church. I could actually list a whole lot of them. Why? There are many reasons, however, the main reason I would like to focus on is revealed in **Genesis: 3:16**: and in the writings of Apostle Paul who wrote of the very reason this curse came upon the woman.

I Timothy 2:14

Adam was not deceived, but the woman being deceived was

119

in the transgression..

Therefore, it was not Adam that was the transgressor, it was the woman. Satan beguiled the woman and she gave unto the man and he did eat. The curse remains with the woman until today.

IN SORROW SHE SHALL BRING FORTH

Genesis 3:16

Unto the woman he said, I will greatly multiply your sorrow and conception: In sorrow thou shalt bring forth children; and thy desire shall be to thy husband, and he shall rule over thee.

Chapter 14

SAVED IN CHILDBEARING

The only way a woman can come out from under this curse is when God fills her with the baptism of the Holy Ghost and she walks uprightly before him.

I Timothy 2:15.

Notwithstanding, she shall be saved in childbearing, if they continue in the faith and charity and holiness with sobriety.

I have heard people say that this Scripture means that a woman who dies giving birth will go to heaven. This is not true! Apostle Paul is saying that the woman is saved by continuing in the faith with charity, holiness and sobriety. It is not because she brought that child forth.

Ephesians 4:5
In Faith (Holiness):

One Lord, [Jesus Christ]*One Faith,* [Holiness]*One baptism* [the Holy Ghost].

I Corinthians 13:13
In Charity [love]: Apostle Paul said:

And now abideth faith, hope, charity, these three; but the greatest of these is charity.

I Peter 5:8
In Sobriety

Be sober, be viligant; because your adversary the devil, as a roaring lion, walketh about, seeking whom he may devour:

The women must also be sober in conversation. Jesus said:

St. Matthew 5:37
But let your communication be, Yea, yea; Nay, nay; for whatsoever is more than these cometh of evil.

Anyone can bring forth a child into the world. Prostitutes and bi-sexuals can bring children into the world and they are not saved, simply because they bring forth a child, even unto death. It does not hold water.

One of the things that took place with my wife is this: She had four children before she received the baptism of the Holy Ghost and two children after she received the baptism. The first four childbirth experiences were different from the latter. With the last two children, my wife had no pain, no misery and no sorrow. According to the word of God, the births were altogether different. I was very much aware of it. My wife felt fine. During the time of her pregnancy, with the last baby, she was working in her flower bed in the yard. I questioned her as to why she went into the yard everyday. She assured me that she was feeling good. After months of working in the yard, she just barely made it to the hospital. Our son, Seth, came with no pain. Indeed there was a big difference. This is why I am confident in the word of God.

The curse is still on the woman today. God's word cannot lie. Humanity can dress it up all they desire to. Some of you might say, just as one of the young ladies said, in our seminar, *"With both of my children, while I was unsaved, (did not have the Holy Ghost) I experienced no pain nor any morning sickness."* I told that this is a rare case but it does happen. The word of God says:

St. Matthew 5:45
...for he maketh his sun to rise on the evil and on the good, and sendeth rain on the just and on the unjust.

This just means that God's blessing can fall on the righteous as well as the unrighteous. This is the mercy and the goodness of God.

My neighbor, who was an unbeliever,(Did not have the Holy Spirit) said that he was a one-woman man and under no circumstances would he have relations with another woman. When his wife died, he waited. Eventually, he got married again. This man wasn't saved. As a matter of fact, he was a long way from being saved. He didn't even want to talk about God. Yet, we have other men that are saved, some are even preachers, but, they are whoremongers. What I am saying is that you cannot put everyone in the same category. Remember it rains on the just (righteous) as well as on the unjust (unrighteous).

Chapter 15

SILLY WOMEN

When God voiced the curse upon the woman He meant just what he said. Let us take a look at the writings of Apostle Paul and see what he had to say about this:

II Timothy 3:1-7.
This know also, that in the last days perilous times shall come. For men shall be lovers of their own selves, covetous, boasters, proud, blasphemers, disobedient to parents, unthankful, unholy, Without natural affection, trucebreakers, false accusers, incontinent, fierce despisers of those that are good, Traitors, heady, highminded, lovers of pleasures more than lovers of God; Having a form of godliness, but denying the power thereof: from such turn away. For this sort are they which creep into houses, and lead captive silly women laden with sins, led away with divers lust, Ever learning, and never able to come to the knowledge of the truth.

Understand what Apostle Paul was saying about the "silly women every learning and never able to come to the knowledge of the truth." The proof is in the pudding. It is a fact that men can wrap **some** women around their fingers over and over. Some men have admitted to sleeping with 1600 to 2,000 women. From this one can see the mood of the women in society today. When you witness a popular group come into town, look and see who it is doing all the

125

screaming and hollering at the musicians, the politicians or the singing groups. The majority of the time it is the women! This is why women are an easy prey and why so many get pregnant out of wedlock. It is sad to say, but, I find it to be fact that most women are easy to be deceived.

Another fact regarding women is this, a woman looks for love. With some women all you have to do is cuddle them and love them. To these women, this is better than sexual intercourse. On the other hand, the man would rather have the sex. The men are not persons that want to do a lot of cuddling. It is different. Normally the female looks for the cuddling, tenderness and to be right up under the man. Very few women can get away from that. Why? It is because of the mothering nature. Women look for love. They have a mothering nature. Due to the mothering nature in the woman, most every woman wants a baby. Very rarely will you find a woman that does not want a child. It is a rare case when you find a woman who does not want children, I do not say that it is not so. It is just rare.

What is the mothering nature? It is simply this: Just as you would nourish a baby, the average woman wants just that. She needs it. She thrives on it. When a woman knows that she has security with her man, she would not care if she lived in a tin can. Ask the woman that lives in a palace and is not receiving that love, what she would rather have and notice her response. Every woman would take that love, that care. She needs it to thrive and to develop. The man does not, remember the nature that God gave man. God gave him dominion over the fish in the sea, over the birds of the air and over every living thing, therefore, a man has a different nature. People try to say that there is no difference between a man and a women; that they are the same and that women and men think alike, however, let me ask this question. How can a man and woman think alike when the woman's body is a factory to produce and the man's is not? How can the woman and the man think alike, when God gave the man dominion and the woman is subject to the man?

Genesis 3:16.
...and thy desire shall be to thy husband and he shall rule over thee.

Again, I ask, how can we think alike? Man is shrewd with a Satanic way about him. He wants his cake and to eat it too. This is contrary to the ways of God. When you look at society and even the churches, you see the contrast.

Although a woman may be filled with the Holy Ghost, she still cannot let her heart direct her. If she follows her heart, she will get into trouble. She has got to follow her mind.

Philippians 2:5.
Let this mind be in you which was also in Christ Jesus.

Chapter 16

HUSBAND LOVE YOUR WIVES

It is a fact that the mother wants to be a mother and the man says he is a "father." To be a father is to be a caretaker. To be a caretaker means shouldering the responsibility. There is a weight on the shoulders of a father which he has to carry. Men, in general, like to be cared for. When a man is really hooked, and I mean, really falls in love, the woman has his heart. However, at the same time that she may have his heart, there is another part of him that hollers out, "I don't want the responsibility." Very few men will step out and really be men and at the same time be tender, loving and look at the needs of a woman. By nature men are selfish. This is the reason why in holiness churches you see more women than men. However the militant organizations called churches is where you will find mostly men.

Take a look at the Muslims. Men go for anything that seems to be macho or masculine. Men look at the army and their first desire is to be a part of the army. Yet, they do not want anyone to tell them what to do. The good man takes care of his family. He may fight with his wife every day, but, he is in love. What kind of love is it? This is where the struggle comes in, and Satan knows it. Let us examine a caring, loving, good man. This is a man who loves his wife, takes care of his children and his family. He will even wash the dishes, make up the bed, cook and let his wife sleep, but, there is something about this person. Once you get to know him and he begins to express himself, you will find that there is something down deep that causes him to walk on the edge. This is one of the reason why so many women are having trouble with their husbands. This should not be, because we can conquer our feelings.

Some people ask me, "Bishop, do you cook," I tell them "Sure, I do. I make up beds and I wash dishes." I don't have a problem with that, however, I am a long way from being a henpecked husband or man. I am still a man in my house. Wherever I go, I am a man who cannot be pushed around. This is very important.

I have again placed here the Scripture in which Apostle Paul speaks about silly women:

II Timothy 3:7
...silly women, laden with sins, led away with divers lust, Ever learning and never able to come to the knowledge of the truth.

This says much about the women, however, when the husband uses his authority as a means of control, he must be also be mindful of the following Scripture.

Ephesians 5:25.
Husband love your wives, even as Christ also loved the church, and gave himself for it.

Therefore, we see that this is a two-way street. God never made it one-sided, but we are living in the midst of much animosity and hatred.

Chapter 17

THE LONELY WOMAN

One demon that primarily attacks females is loneliness. Because of the way females are raised, some women feel if they don't have a man, it is the worst thing in the world that can happen to them. This is where the demons take advantage. Some will even go as far to say that half a man is better than no man; meaning they will take what they can get.

Another cause of concern is this: Very rarely do you hear people say to the boys "Who is your girlfriend?" The little boy is out there playing with trucks. It is not the men asking this question of the little boys, rather it is the women asking the little girls, "Who is your boyfriend?" I have heard it many times, even in our churches. What is being said causes the little children as early as three or four years of age to become aware of boyfriends and girlfriends. After awhile the little dolls become babies, the little boys become fathers/husbands and the little girls want to play house. The little boys want to play stickball, but the little girl wants to be mommy and play house.

Every man I know of was taught sex by a girl. Females come into puberty early. Here is a sign. As a rule you never see the little boy pulling on the little girl, but most of the time you see the little girls pulling on the little boys. Some, as they get older, will even hit the boys and run.

While I was in Africa, I witnessed babies with babies. One young lady was only eleven years older than her

131

daughter. This means the young lady got pregnant at the age of 10 after she had come into her puberty. All these things happen to the little girls and they do not fully realize what is happening. It is always to get a boyfriend. As the single young lady gets older, it bothers her not to have a husband, more so than it does the man. The man says "I'm free." One man use to have a saying, "Why should I make one woman miserable, when I can make so many women happy," therefore, men find mates like vultures. Through sexual contact the woman gets part of that man. The man cohabitates and he is finished. He has gotten what he wanted and he is fine. He doesn't have to come back. The woman says, "Do you love me?" They laugh at the virgin and make vulgar comments.

Satan takes advantage of our ignorance through our sexual organ or our liberal attitude toward sex. The worst thing an woman can do, is to let a man have his free will with her. She may feel by giving in she will keep him. However, he is satisfied sexually without the responsibility. Try and keep him and she will lose him

Chapter 18

THERE IS NEITHER MALE
NOR FEMALE IN CHRIST JESUS

Satan has bound many women physically and mentally. We are aware of this, however, many women are also bound spiritually because of church doctrine. Let me give you a perfect example. A minister had been coming to me for counseling and he was leaning toward me and moving away from certain doctrines in his organization. When he heard about the demonology services he desired to come. He stated that he was a contractor and his wife was a nurse. They both had jobs, but it seem like they could not keep any money. He convinced his wife to come to the demonology service and he asked me to call out the demon of poverty.

When I called the demon of poverty, his wife advanced down the aisle toward me. She was hunched over and the spirit sounded like a grizzly bear. I told my workers to leave her alone, because when she came she would kneel at my feet and I would cast the demon out of her. That is exactly what she did. The demon drove her down the aisle and right to where I was standing. She kneeled at my feet and I cast the demon out of her. She later remarked that she had never seen anything like it although it happened to her. Therefore, when her husband died, she trusted me enough to call me to preach her husband's funeral. The woman was in bondage in her church. Apostle Paul made it plain in the Scriptures:

Galatians 3:26-28
For ye are all the children of God by faith in Christ Jesus. For as many of you as have been baptized into Christ [by the Holy Ghost] *have put on Christ. There is neither Jew nor Greek, there is neither bond nor free, there is <u>neither male nor female</u>: for ye are all one in Christ Jesus.*

When I went to this large organization to preach. I preached the word of God unadulterated. One of the bishops, almost one-hundred years old grabbed me and said, "This is the way it should be." Another came and hugged me and said, "I want to come to your church." However, all the rest of those men, everyone of them walked by and ignored me. They did not speak to me, or acknowledge the message. Instead they walked by me in anger. Talk about demons, this was it, but the women were happy after hearing the message. It was something in that church with the women. They were in bondage under those men, however, when they heard the gospel unadulterated, it gave them joy. The truth is the light.

St. John 8:32
And ye shall know the truth, and the truth shall make you free.

One of those same men was the one who came when we were setting up our Church in Mt. Vernon, New York. He came walking around with a couple of his associates and said, "You came to Mt. Vernon. Why didn't you ask us? Did you ask any of the ministers, if you could come to Mt. Vernon? I have the biggest Pentecostal church in Mt. Vernon. Who gave you the authority?" I said to him God told me to come that the people of God might have an alternative. God always proves himself. We came to our big sanctuary with just fourteen people. Now our churches are full.

PART VII

SATAN MOTIVATES

THE FIRST FAMILY

Chapter 19

THE BIRTH OF CAIN AND ABEL

In the Book of Genesis we are introduced to the family of Adam.

Genesis 4:1-2

And Adam knew Eve his wife; and she conceived, and bare Cain, and said, I have gotten a man from the Lord. And she again bare his brother Abel. And Abel was a keeper of the sheep, but Cain was a tiller of the ground.

THEIR WORKS BY THEIR FAITH
Genesis 4:3-5

And in process of time it came to pass, that Cain brought of the fruit of the ground an offering unto the Lord. And Abel, he also brought of the firstlings of his flock and of the fat thereof. And the Lord had respect unto Abel and to his offering. But unto Cain and to his offering he had not respect;

THE MOTIVATOR - DEMONS OF ANGER, JEALOUSLY, COVETEOUSNESS

Genesis 4:6

And Cain was very wroth and his countenance fell. And the Lord said unto Cain, Why art thy wroth? and Why is thy countenance fallen?

Here we see that both brothers have offered up an offering unto the Lord. This was their works and their faith in action. Abel took of the best, the fatling of the flock, and offered it unto God. But Cain was a tiller of the ground, therefore, he took of his fruit and his vegetables. But God did not accept his offering because it was not a blood offering. Here we find that after Cain's countenance was fallen, he became angry. God's word says:

NEITHER GIVE PLACE TO THE DEVIL
Genesis 4:7
If thou doest well, shalt thou not be accepted? and if thou doest not well, sin lieth at the door. And unto thee shall be his desire, and thou shalt rule over him.

Notice that the word says, sin lieth at the door. Let us put it this way, the Devil lies at the door. There is an old saying, "Whom the gods destroyed, they first made angry." Cain being angry was in the position for Satan to work. In other words we must not give Satan an open door. The Scriptures says:

Ephesians 4:27
neither give place to the devil.

Once we give the Devil an open door, he will come in to work. Here the Lord is saying that sin shall rule over him; meaning that sin would be his portion. All of this and more took place here all because Satan, the Motivator was on the job.

DEMONS OF MURDER AND LYING
IN THE FIRST FAMILY
Genesis 4:8-10
And Cain talked with Abel, his brother: and it came to pass, when they were in the field, that Cain rose up against Abel his brother, and slew him. And the Lord said unto

Cain, Where is Abel thy brother? And he said, I know not: Am I my brother's keeper? And he said, What hast thou done? the voice of thy brother's blood crieth unto me from the ground.

2ᴺᴰ GENERATION CURSED
Genesis 4:11-13
And now art thou cursed from the earth, which hath opened her mouth to receive thy brother's blood from thy hand; When thou tillest the ground, it shall not henceforth yeild unto thee her strength; a fugitve and a vagabond shalt thou be in the earth. And Cain said unto the Lord, My punishment is greater than I can bear.

THE CONSEQUENCES OF SIN WORKING IN THE FAMILY

Let us look at the consequences of sin. We see that sin (the devil) caused Adam and Eve to be driven from the garden and Cain was wrought because God would not accept his offering. Cain rose up against his brother and slew him. Punishment was upon him and he cried out, *"My punishment is greater that I can bear."*

Satan, the Motivator, did not tell him what the consequences would be, but, he drove him to this act. We see Satan moving and working, his job is to destroy and again, the word of God has reached its mark.

I Corinthians 15:22
For as in Adam all die, even so in Christ shall all be made alive.

Due to the fact that Satan tempted Eve and she gave unto Adam and he did eat, we find sin at work in the entire

141

family back in the beginning. The consequences of sin can affect our entire family today. It brings about generational curses and again I state that Satan, the Motivator, is working within many of our families.

Chapter 20

CURSES OVER THE FAMILY[6]

Generations of families have been cursed because of sin in the family. One of the sad things that happens is when people blame God for what happens in their lives. Read what God's word says:

Exodus 20:5-6:
For I the Lord thy God am a jealous God, visiting the iniquity of the fathers upon the children unto the third and fourth generation of them that hate me. [Do not keep my commandments] *And shewing mercy unto thousands of them that love me and keep my commandments.*

Many times the father or the mother comes from bad seed and this is because of sin. It may be that the mother and/or father were promiscuous people. Their children do not know God and are not taught to fear God or to respect themselves or others. The family, through many generations, did not honor God. The demons take over the whole family through lasciviousness, vulgarity, drugs, incest, fighting, anger, etc., and it brings about destruction. Little children will become exactly as their mother and father because they did likewise. The demons run rampant in the family.

---

[6] *"Manual On Demonology, Diary of An Exorcist",* Curses Over The Family Chapter 18, page 119." Author Bishop Roy Bryant, Sr., D.D. published by Impact Christian Books, Inc. ISBN #0-89228-123-5

When I visited in mental institutions, it was sad to see the degree of sin upon the unrighteousness. I have never seen such with God-fearing Christian people. During one visit, years ago, in the now closed Willowbrook Mental Institution in the state of New York, I noticed a fine dignified couple sitting with their child. They were heartbroken because of the child's mental state. They said, "We do not understand what caused this." I told them that they were the cause. They did not want to hear anything about their lifestyle and they resented me for making this statement. This is exactly what Jesus meant when He said:

St. Matthew 7:18
...neither can a corrupt tree bring forth good fruit.

It is strange when we hear a whole generation being taught, "Do not deprive your child," or "Let the child express himself as he wishes." Many generations were raised this way and are now ruling over their parents. Read what the word of God has to say regarding this:

Isaiah 3:5, 12.
And the people shall be oppressed, every one by another, and every one by his neighbour: the child shall behave himself proudly against the ancient, and the base against the honourable. As for my people, children are the oppressors, and the women rule over them. O my people, they which lead thee cause thee to err and destroy the way of thy paths.

God's Word also states:
Proverbs 22:6
Train up a child in the way he should go: and when he is

144

old, he will not depart from it.

We can come out from under the generational curse (curse of inheritance) once we receive the baptism of the Holy Ghost. The word of God states:

II Corinthians 5:17

Therefore if any man be in Christ, [born again] *he is a new creature: old things are passed away; behold, all things are become new.*

Refer also to:

Ezekiel 18:1-5

The word of the Lord came unto me again, saying, What mean ye, that ye use this proverb concerning the land of Israel, saying, The fathers have eaten sour grapes, and the children's teeth are set on edge? As I live, saith the Lord God, ye shall not have occasion any more to use this proverb in Israel. Behold all souls are mine; as the soul of the father, so also the soul of the son is mine: the soul that sinneth, it shall die. But if a man be just and do that which is lawful and right, ...

Verse 17

...he shall not die for the iniquity of his father he shall surely live, saith the Lord God.

What is Ezekiel saying? Formerly, the sins of the fathers (parents) were visited upon the children, and the fathers (parents) were responsible for the sins of the children. But now God is saying this would no longer be the case. Each person would be responsible for his own sins. The righteousness of the righteous shall be upon him and the wickedness of the wicked shall be upon him. Whenever we turn from our sins, God is just and quick to forgive us.

Many people say that they are alcoholics because their parents and/or other family members were alcoholics. Likewise, they are depressed and suicidal because their parents were diagnosed as having a chemical imbalance of the brain and they were suicidal and some were confined to mental institutions. Prison inmates have sons and daughters that are inmates. Drug addicts produce other drug addicts. Curses and sins from grandparents and parents are passed down from one generation to another, however, just as God told Israel, this will no longer be an excuse. No longer will we say we are this way because our fathers have eaten sour grapes (sinned) and our children's teeth are set on edge (bearing the burden of the father's sins.) The Baptism of the Holy Ghost has given us a way out. (Read the 2nd chapter of **Acts,** the 3rd chapter of **St John**.) The Apostle Paul tell us that we are new creatures in Christ Jesus, we no longer have to be **adulterers**, **alcoholics, mentally depressed, suicidal, witches, warlocks, psychics, liars, thieves, drug addicts,** etc.

If you have curses visited upon you from generations ago, deliverance is able to break the curse over you and your family. Jesus Christ is the answer. I have come across the demon of **"curse inheritance over the family"** and I have cast him out on many occasions. These people are now free from bondage.

PART VIII

THE MOTIVATOR

BEHIND

THE WORKS

(*CONTINUED*)

Chapter 21

SATAN MOTIVATES
DAVID TO NUMBER ISRAEL

I Chronicles 21:1-15.

And Satan stood up against Israel, and provoked David to number Israel. And David said to Joab and to the rulers of the people, Go, number Israel from Beersheba even to Dan; and bring the number of them to me, that I may know it. And Joab answered, The Lord make his people an hundred times so many more as they be: but, my Lord the King, are they not all my lord's servants? Why then doth my Lord require this thing? Why will he be a cause of trespass to Israel? Nevertheless the king's word prevailed against Joab. Wherefore Joab departed, and went throughout all Israel, and came to Jerusalem. And Joab gave the sum of the number of the people unto David. And all they of Israel were a thousand thousand and an hundred thousand men that drew sword: and Judah was four hundred threescore and ten thousand men that drew sword. But Levi and Benjamin counted he not among them: for the king's word was abominable to Joab. And God was displeased with this thing; therefore he smote Israel. And David said unto God, I have sinned greatly, because I have done this thing: but now, I beseech thee, do away the iniquity of thy servant; for I have done very foolishly. And the Lord spake unto Gad, David's seer, saying, Go and tell David, saying, Thus saith the Lord, I offer thee three things: choose thee one of them that I may

do it unto thee. So Gad came to David, and said unto him,
Thus saith the Lord, Choose thee. Either three years'
famine; or three months to be destroyed before thy foes,
while that the sword of thine enemies overtaketh thee; or
else three days the sword of the Lord, even the pestilence,
in the land, and the angel of the Lord destroying
throughout all the coasts of Israel. Now therefore advise
thyself what word I shall bring again to him that sent me.
And David said unto Gad, I am in a great strait: let me fall
now into the hand of the LORD; for very great are his
mercies: but let me not fall into the hands of man. So the
Lord sent pestilence upon Israel: and there fell of Israel
seventy thousand men. And God sent an angel unto
Jerusalem to destroy it: and as he was destroying, the
Lord beheld, and he repented him of the evil, and said to
the angel that destroyed, It is enough, stay now thine hand.
And the angel of the Lord stood by the threshingfloor of
Ornan the Jebusite.

I Chronicles 21:16, 17.
And David lifted up his eyes and saw the angel of the Lord
stand between the earth and the heaven, having a drawn
sword in his hand stretched out over Jerusalem. The David
and the elders of Israel, who were clothed in sackcloth, fell
upon their faces. And David said unto God, Is it not I who
commanded the people to be numbered? Even I it is that
have sinned and done evil indeed; but as for these sheep,
what have they done? Let thine hand, I pray thee, O Lord
my God, be on me, and on my father's house, but not on thy
people, that they should be plagued.

Now the plague was stayed from Israel. However, what
we are getting from the very first verse is that Satan stood

up against David to number Israel. Joab tried to talk him out of it. But Satan was the motivator and David was angry with his servant, the captain of the host. David wanted him to go forth and number Israel. In other words, what business is it of yours? the captain of the host said. Is it yours or mine? God has blessed Israel and multiplied them greatly. Why even bother with the number. It is a waste of time and effort. Yet, David did not want to hear what his servant had to say. When Satan is the motivator, he continues to press and press until we find ourselves in a great strait and we are not able to function. Why because Satan is there. The Bible says:

Romans 6:16

Know ye not that to whom ye yield yourselves servants to obey, his servants ye are to whom ye obey; whether of sin unto death, or of obedience unto righteousness.

Since David yielded himself to obey Satan. Satan, in this instance got the victory. In the plague, God moved that he might destroy Israel. David would run before his enemies and David knew very well that his enemies desired his life. You see the works of Satan. This is why we call this book, *Satan, The Motivator* because Satan is in back of the work.

Romans 6:16

Know you not that to whom you yield yourselves servants to obey, his servants you are to whom you obey; whether of sin unto death, or of obedience unto righteousness?

152

Chapter 22

SATAN, THE MOTIVATOR BEHIND THE WORKS OF KING OF TYRE.

Let us now read Ezekiel, Chapter 28. This is a chapter that I find many people having a lot of trouble with. Ezekiel 28, starts out with the rebuke of the King of Tyre. Tyre was a seaport town where much traffic came in and went out. God rebuked the king of Tyre, however, we are after the motivator of the King, which is most important. Let us read a portion of this. I want you to read along with me, because this is a teaching series. Keep in mind the King of Tyre and who is behind him.

DANIEL THE WISE MAN.
Ezekiel 28:3
Behold, thou art wiser than Daniel; there is no secret that they can hide from thee:

The word of God is talking about Satan, when he said, "thou art wiser than Daniel." It would be impossible for the King of Tyrus, himself, to be wiser than Daniel, because God had given Daniel, wisdom, knowledge and to understand mysteries and dreams.

Let us read **Daniel 1:17:**
As for these four children (Shadrach, Meshach, Abednego, and Daniel) God gave them knowledge and skill in all learning and wisdom: and Daniel had understanding in all visions and dreams.

153

God gave gifts unto Daniel and he was a wise man. He had sense enough to serve God and he saved his soul alive.

Chapter 23

GOD'S CREATED BEING

Let us continue with:

Ezekiel 28:2-12:

Son of man, say unto the prince of Tyrus, Thus saith the Lord God; Because thine heart is lifted up, and thou hast said, I am a God, I sit in the seat of God, in the midst of the seas, yet thou art a man, and not God, though thy set thine heart as the heart of God: Behold thy art wiser than Daniel; there is no secret that they can hide from thee: With thy wisdom and with thine understanding thou hast gotten thee riches, and hast gotten gold and silver into thy treasures. By thy great wisdom and by thy traffick has thou increased thy riches, and thine heart is lifted up because of thy riches: Therefore, thus saith the Lord God: Because thou has set thine heart as the heart of God; Behold, therefore, I will bring strangers upon thee, the terrible of the nations; and they shall draw their swords against the beauty of thy wisdom, and they shall defile thy brightness. They shall bring thee down to the pit, and thou shalt die the deaths of them that are slain in the midst of the seas. Wilt thou yet say before him that slayeth thee, I am God? But thou shalt be a man, and no God, in the hand of him that slayeth thee. Thou shalt die the deaths of the uncircumcised by the hand of strangers: for I have spoken it, saith the Lord God. Moreover, the word of the Lord came unto me, saying, Son of man, take up a lamentation upon the king of Tyrus and say unto him, Thus saith the Lord God: Thy sealest up the sum, full of wisdom and perfect in beauty.

155

Here, I will pause, because this is where so much confusion comes from. God is talking to the King of Tyrus, but he is looking beyond the King of Tyrus to the *Motivator*, the one that caused the problem to exist. Remember, Satan offered Jesus the Kingdom of this world, if he would bow down and worship him. (St. Matthew 4th chapter). What he was doing was offering Jesus the riches of the world. The Bible calls Satan "The God of this World" and the "Prince of the Air." Notice the word is pointing directly at Satan.

Ezekiel 28:12

Son of man, take up a lamentation upon the king of Tyrus, and say unto him, Thus saith the Lord God; Thou sealest up the sum, full of wisdom and perfect in beauty. Thou has been in Eden in the garden of God; every precious stone was thy covering, the sardius, topaz and the diamond, the beryl, the onyx, and the jasper, the sapphire, the emerald, and the carbuncle, and gold: the workmanship of thy tabrets and of thy pipes prepared in thee in the day that thou wast created.

Here we find that God was talking about a created being. Let us continue reading:

Ezekiel 28:14-19

Thou art the anointed cherub that covereth, and I have set thee so; thou wast upon the holy mountain of God; thou has walked up and down in the midst of the stones of fire. Thou was perfect in thy ways from the day that wast created, till inquity was found in thee. By the multitude of thy merchandise they have filled the midst of thee with violence, and thou has sinned: therefore, I will cast thee as profane out of the mountain of God; and I will destroy thee,

O covering cherub, from the midst of the stones of fire. Thine heart was lifted up because of thy beauty; thou has corrupted thy wisdom by reason of thy brightness; I will cast thee to the ground, I will lay thee before kings, that they may behold thee. Thou has defiled thy sanctuaries by the multitude of thine iniquities, by the iniquity of thy traffick; therefore will I bring forth a fire from the midst of thee, it shall devour thee, and I will bring thee to ashes upon the earth in the sight of all them that behold thee. All they that know thee among the people shall be astonished at thee; thou shalt be a terror, and never shalt thou be any more.

THE JUDGMENT OF SATAN, THE MOTIVATOR

God went on to describe the judgment, when Satan shall be shackled and put into the bottomless pit of hell and eventually cast into the lake of fire.

Revelation 20:1, 20:10

And I saw an angel come down from heaven, having the key of the bottomless pit and a great chain in his hand. And he laid hold on the dragon, that old serpent, which is the Devil, and Satan, and bound him a thousand years. And the Devil that deceived them was cast into the lake of fire and brimstone, where the beast and the false prophet are, and shall be tormented day and night forever and ever.

Satan was created perfect. People often ask where did the lies start. They started in Satan, himself.

Ezekiel 28:15

Thou was perfect in thy ways from the day that thou was created, till iniquity was found in thee.

Chapter 24

SATAN, THE MOTIVATOR, AND JOB

Let us refer to Job and see Satan, The Motivator. Now remember he motivated Adam and Eve, Cain to slay Abel, David to number the people and also the king of Tyrus. Again we find the motivator again at work.

Job 1:1
There was a man in the land of Uz, whose name was Job; and that man was perfect and upright, and one that feared God and eschewed evil.

The old question remains; why must the righteous suffer? Let us read Job 1:6 and see the motivator at work causing the righteous to suffer.

Job 1:6
Now there was a day when the sons of God came to present themselves before the Lord, and Satan came also among them.

This was the permissible will of God. Satan had already been cast out of heaven. At this time God calls the sons together, (a celestial gathering) and Satan came also in the midst of them. Satan could not enter into the abode of God, which is the 3rd heaven. **Revelation 12:7** and **Isaiah 14:12** tells us that he was cast out of heaven. This brief meeting was in the air Let us read further in the Scriptures beginning at the 7th verse:

Job 1:7-12

And the Lord said unto Satan, Whence comest thou? Then Satan answered the Lord, and said, From going to and fro in the earth, and from walking up and down in it. And the Lord said unto Satan, Hast thou considered my servant Job, there is none like him in the earth, a perfect and an upright man, one that feareth God, and escheweth evil? Then Satan answered the Lord and said, Doth Job fear God for nought? Hast not thou made an hedge about him, and about his house, and about all that he hath on every side? thou hast blessed the work of his hands, and his substance is increased in the land. But put forth thine hand now, and touch all that he hath, and he will curse thee to thy face. And the Lord said unto Satan, Behold all that he hath is in thy power; only upon himself put not forth thine hand. So Satan went forth from the presence of the Lord.

Now this is the battle! Satan, the motivator, challenging God. Did Job serve God for nothing? Why do we serve God? We have our reasons. Satan accused God of having a hedge (protection) around Job, and he could not get to him. In other words Satan told God, "You have been protecting him all of these years. Take that hedge from around him and let me get to him. The Lord allowed Satan to go ahead and touch him and all that he had. Let us read a little further:

Job 1:13-17

And there was a day when his sons and daughters were eating and drinking wine in their eldest brother's house: And there came a messenger unto Job, and said, The oxen

160

were plowing, and the asses feeding beside them: And the Sabeans fell upon them, and took them away; yea, they have slain the servants with the edge of the sword; and I only am escaped alone to tell thee.

The word of God goes on to tell us that Job lost everything. In other words God told Satan. "you may touch all his possessions." Let us look at the 16th verse:

While he was yet speaking, there came also another, and said, The fire of God is fallen from heaven, and hath burned up the sheep, and the servants, and consumed them; and I only am escaped alone to tell thee. While he was yet speaking, there came also another, and said, The fire of God is fallen from heaven, and hath burned up the sheep, and the servants, and consumed them; and I only am escaped alone to tell thee. Then Job arose, and rent his mantle, and shaved his head, and fell down upon the ground, and worshipped. And said, Naked came I out of my mother's womb, and naked shall I return thither: the LORD gave, and the LORD hath taken away; blessed be the name of the Lord. In all this Job sinned not, nor charged God foolishly.

Notice that God allowed Satan to touch all that he had; all his material goods, his family and such. We see after this had taken place, Job worshipped God. Job's prayer, worship, praising and trusting God was his strength.

Job 2:1-3
Again there was a day when the sons of God came to present themselves before the Lord, and Satan came also among them to present himself before the Lord. And the

161

Lord said unto Satan, From whence comest thou? And Satan answered the Lord, and said, From going to and fro in the earth and from walking up and down in it. And the Lord said unto Satan, Hast thou considered my servant Job, that there is none like him in the earth, a perfect and an upright man, one that feareth God, and escheweth evil? and still he holdeth fast his integrity, although thou movedst me against him, to destroy him without cause.

Observe that the Lord told Satan, "You moved me against my servant Job without a cause. In other words, I had no cause to do this to Job.

SATAN, THE MOTIVATOR, CAUSES AFFLICTION

Job 2:4-8

And Satan answered the Lord, and said, Skin for skin, yea, all that a man hath will he give for his life. But put forth thine hand now, and touch his bone and his flesh and he curse thee to thy face. And the Lord said unto Satan, Behold, he is in thine hand; but save his life. [In other words do what you so desire, but you cannot take the breath of life out of his body.] *So went Satan forth from the presence of the Lord, and smote Job with sore boils from the sole of his foot unto his crown. And he took a potsherd to scrape himself withal and he sat down with the ashes.*

Let us look at the next move of Satan, The Motivator.

SATAN MOTIVATES JOB'S WIFE
Job 2:9

Then said his wife unto him, Dost thou still retain thine

162

integrity? curse God, and die.

Now isn't this amazing? God allowed Satan to take away his family, all his material wealth and he touched his body. After all this suffering and his wife states "Why don't you curse God and die." Here was Job's answer.

A FOOLISH WOMAN AND A WISE HUSBAND

Job 2:10

But he said unto her, Thou speakest as one of the foolish women speaketh. What? shall we receive good at the hand of God, and shall not we receive evil? In all this did not Job sin with his lips.

This is Satan, the Motivator, at work moving God against his servant, Job. I bring this study on Satan, The Motivator, because so many times we say, I don't know what is happening to me. But many times we believe or at least we attributed it to Satan.

Let us go to the 109th division of Psalms and let us see what the Psalmist has to say. Here we find another of God's people suffering.

Chapter 25

SATAN MOTIVATES LIARS

Psalms 109:1-2
Hold not thy peace, O God of my praise; For the mouth of the wicked and the mouth of the deceitful are opened against me: they have spoken against me with a lying tongue.

Notice here the lies that are spoken against God's servant. The Bible says that Satan is the father of lies. Therefore, he is motivating enemies to speak against the psalmist.

Look at what the Gospel has to say about Satan:

St. John 8:44
He was a murderer from the beginning, and abode not in the truth, because there is no truth in him. When he speaketh a lie, he speaketh of his own; for he is a liar and the father of it.

SATAN MOTIVATES PEOPLE
Let us continue to read the 109th divison of Psalms and the 3rd Verse:

Psalms 109:3-10
They compassed me about also with words of hatred; and fought against me without a cause. For my love they are my adversaries: but I give myself unto prayer. And they have rewarded me evil for good, and hatred for my love. Set thou a wicked man over him: and let Satan stand at his

right hand. When he shall be judged, let him be condemned: and let his prayer become sin. Let his days be few; and let another take his office. Let his children be fatherless, and his wife a widow. Let his children be continually vagabonds and beg: let them seek their bread also out of their desolate places.

What we see here is how Satan motivates people to work against us. I believe the psalmist is David. You notice he said they hated me without a cause. For my love they are my adversaries. David was a man of great love and a praying man also. He said, "but I give myself unto prayer." Remember David would not touch Saul because Saul was God's anointed. David loved his family very much. However, in this Scripture David is saying, "Let his wife be a widow and his children be fatherless." In other words kill him, he is asking God for the death of the man. Therefore, we see sometimes Satan can oppress us. We can wish these things upon our enemies.

Chapter 26

THE MOTIVATOR
OPPRESSES THE RIGHTEOUS

Satan oppresses the righteous. If we again observe the trial of Job we can see how he questioned and cursed the day he was born; he cursed the womb that gave him life; he cursed the man that brought the news that a man child was born.

Job 3:1-3, 11
After this opened Job his mouth, and cursed his day. And Job spake, and said, Let the day perish wherein I was born, and the night in which it was said, There is a man child conceived. Why died I not from the womb? why did I not give up the ghost when I came out of the belly?

Job was very much vexed. Satan can bring us to a state of vexation and cause us to cry out to God. He (Satan) tries to wear out the patience of the saints. He gets us so tired sometimes that we just wish to give up and say, "Lord, I can't go on any futher." By the grace of God are we protected from evil. Let us remember the patience of Job:

James 5:11
Behold, we count them happy which endure. Ye have heard of the patience of Job, and have seen the end of the Lord; that the Lord is very pitiful, and of tender mercy.

The Apostle Paul besought the Lord thrice that his thorn in the flesh might depart from him. God gave him this answer.

II Corinthians 12:9

...my grace is sufficient for thee: for my strength is made perfect in weakness.

Chapter 27

SATAN RESISTS
JOSHUA THE HIGH PRIEST

Zachariah 3:1-7:

And he shewed me Joshua the high priest standing before the angel of the Lord, and Satan standing at his right hand to resist him. [This Joshua is not Moses' companion, Joshua the son of Nun.] *And the Lord said unto Satan, The Lord rebuke thee Satan, O Satan, the Lord that hath chosen Jerusalem rebuke thee: is not this a brand plucked out to the fire? Now Joshua was clothed with filthy garments, and stood before the angel. And he answered and spake unto those that stood before him, saying, Take away the filthy garments from him. And unto him he said, Behold, I have caused thine iniquity to pass from thee, and I will clothe thee with a change of raiment. And I said, Let them set a fair mitre upon his head. So they set a fair mitre upon his head, and clothed him with garments. And the angel of the Lord stood by. And the angel of the Lord protested unto Joshua, saying, Thus saith the Lord of hosts; if thou wilt walk in my ways, and if thou wilt keep my charge, then thou shalt also judge my house, and shalt also keep my courts, and I will give thee places to walk among these that stand by.*

What is happening is that Joshua, had on filthy garments, which is unrighteousness. God is cleansing Joshua and preparing him that he might be able to stand before God. God is saying to walk upright before me. In other words, I will bless thee and I will be with thee. You will notice even before God cleansed Joshua the High Priest that Satan was standing before him to resist him. We know What happens when God put his Spirit in us. Here we are now Christians with Satan standing right beside us. God had changed our garments from unrighteousness to his righteousness and Satan was right there. We know what is happening in our lives. Just as Satan resisted the high priest then, so it is with us today. Satan, the motivator, is at work.

Chapter 28

THE MOTIVATOR OF THE TEMPTATION IN THE WILDERNESS

Let us go to another Scripture that may be a little more familiar to you. We will look in the Gospel of St. Matthew chapter 4 in our New Testament. No doubt many of us have heard quite a bit about the "temptation in the wilderness." The Holy Spirit is a tester and this was a time of testing. The Spirit of God drove Jesus into the wilderness, whereby, that he might be tested. Let us look at what the word says:

St. Matthew 4:1-3
Then was Jesus led up of the Spirit into the wilderness to be tempted of the devil. And when he had fasted forty days and forty nights, he was afterward an hungered. And when the tempter came to him, he said, If thou be the Son of God, command that these stones be made bread.

Notice Satan said: "if thou be the Son of God." Again we find Satan at work. Satan knew very well Jesus was hungry and desired to eat. Nevertheless, Satan tempted him by saying, "Go ahead turn these stones into bread."

Satan also knew that Jesus is the Son of God, personified in the flesh. In other words Satan said, "Now, if you are the Son of God, prove it. I know you can do it, but go ahead, if you be the Son of God." Sometimes Satan will challenge us the same way. Through the word of God we can get the victory. Jesus answered Satan with the

171

written word.

St. Matthew 4:4-5
But he [Jesus] answered him [Satan] and said, It is written, Man shall not live by bread alone, but by every word that proceedeth out of the mouth of God. Then the devil taketh him up into the holy city, and setteth him on a pinnacle of the temple.

We must remember that this is the permissible will of God. In other words, God allowed Satan to take him up to the pinnacle of the temple. He allowed Satan to tempt Jesus.

St. Matthew 4:6
And saith unto him. If thou be the son of God, cast thyself down: for it is written, He shall give his angels charge concerning thee: and in their hands they shall bear thee up, lest at any time thy dash thy foot against a stone.

Again we witness Satan saying, "if thou be the son of God..." and Jesus using the written word.

St. Matthew 4:7-11
Jesus said unto him, It is written again, Thou shalt not tempt the Lord thy God. Again the devil taketh him up into an exceeding high mountain and showed him all the kingdoms of the world, and the glory of them; And saith unto him. All these things will I give thee, if thou wilt fall down and worship me. Then saith Jesus unto him, Get thee hence Satan: for it is written, Thou shalt worship the Lord thy God, and him only shall thy serve. Then the devil leaveth him, and, behold, angels came and ministered unto

him.

In other words, the Devil left him for just a short period of time. The Devil doesn't go very far very often. When he does it is only for a period of time. Notice in the mist of all these temptations Jesus was meeting the test on every hand. The Devil will always be trying to stop the Lord's work.

This is the same Devil, a/k/a Lucifer, that we read about in the book of **Ezekiel, chapter 28** and the same Devil, a/k/a the tail of the Dragon, that was cast out of heaven in **Revelation 7**. Now we see Satan offering Jesus all the kingdoms of the world. Yet, God controls the world. However, Satan is the god of this world, the prince of the air and the motivator of temptation.

Jesus was tempted, tried and tested. How then shall we escape? Many times our testing will take us through great trials and tribulations. However, because Jesus endured temptations, he can be touched by our infirmities. Again, I will go back to the word to supports my statements:

OUR HIGH PRIEST
Hebrews 4:15-16.
For we have not an high priest which cannot be touched with the feelings of our infirmities : but was in all points tempted like as we are yet with sin. Let us therefore come boldly to the throne of grace that we may obtain mercy, and find grace to help in the time of need.

ABRAHAM TESTED
The Bible speaks about how Abraham was tested. God told Abraham to offer up his only son upon the altar as a sacrifice unto him.

Genesis 22:1-2

And it came to pass after these things, that God did tempt Abraham, [meaning tested] *and said unto him, Abraham: and he said, Behold, here I am. And he said, Take now thy son, thine only son Issac, whom thou lovest, and get thee into the land of Moriah; and offer him there for a burnt offering upon one of the mountains which I will tell thee of.*

By reading another portion of Genesis 22nd chapter, we will see how Abraham passed the test.

Genesis 22:3, 10-12

And Abraham rose up early in the morning, and saddled his ass, and took two of his young men with him, and Isaac his son, and clave the wood for the burnt offering, and rose up, and went into the place of which God had told him. And Abraham stretched forth his hand, and took the knife to slay his son. And the angel of the Lord called unto him out of heaven, and said, Abraham, Abraham: and he said, Here am I. And he said, Lay not thine hand upon the lad, neither do thou any thing unto him: for now I know that thou fearest God, seeing thou hast not withheld thy son, thine only son from me.

The word of God proves to us that God does not tempt. He tests us, but he does not tempt us with evil. Temptation is the works of the flesh and the works of Satan. Let us read:

James 1:12-16

Blessed is the man that endureth temptation; for when he is tried, he shall receive the crown of life, which the Lord hath promised to them that love him. Let no man say when he is tempted of God: for God cannot be tempted with evil,

174

neither tempteth he any man: But every man is tempted, when he is drawn away of his own lust and enticed. Then when lust is conceived, it bringeth forth sin: and sin, when it is finished, bringeth forth death. Do not err, my beloved brethren.

I Corinthians 10:13:

There hath no temptation taken you but such as is common to man: but God is faithful, who will not suffer you to be tempted above that ye are able; but will with the temptation also make a way to escape, that ye may be able to bear it.

Chapter 29

BLIND, DUMB AND DEAF SPIRITS WORKING WITH THE MOTIVATOR

St. Matthew 12:22:
Then was brought unto him one possessed with a devil, blind, and dumb: and he healed him, insomuch that the blind and dumb both spoke and saw.

Here we find that Satan afflicted this man: the word says possessed with a devil. Therefore, it does not have to be the Devil, himself. There is only one Lucifer. This was a blind spirit and a dumb spirit. Satan has an awful lot of demons (also known as devils) working with him. We ask the question:

WHERE DID THEY COME FROM?
The same place Satan came from; heaven.
Revelation 12:9:
...Satan was cast out into the earth, and his angels were cast out with him.

Those that followed Satan in the rebellion were those that were working with him. Jesus was accused of casting out devils by Belzeebulb, the prince of the devils. In other words by the Devil. The Lord let them know that he cast out devils by the finger of God.

SATAN'S KINGDOM IS NOT DIVIDED
Jesus said:

St. Matthew 12:25-26.

A Kingdom divided against itself shall not stand. Every kingdom divided against itself is brought to desolation; and every city or house divided against itself shall not stand. And if Satan cast out Satan, he is divided against himself; how shall his kingdom stand?

Satan's kingdom is certainly not divided. You cannot take the Devil and cast out the devil. It is God casting out these evil spirits in the name of Jesus. This is the only way it works. It just does not work any other way. Some times we, Christians, are divided one against another; one church fighting another church; one preacher fighting against another preacher. We are all divided. There is also an awful lot of jealousy amongst the people of God. Not so with the Devil! Therefore his kingdom remains strong because he is not divided. Just imagine if we, the Lord's people, were as united together as the Devil's people. We would be in great shape.

AN OPEN DOOR FOR SATAN, THE MOTIVATOR
St. Luke 11:24-28:

When an unclean spirit is gone out of a man, he walketh through dry places seeking rest; and findeth none, he saith, I will return unto my house whence I came out. And when he cometh, he findeth it swept and garnished. Then goeth he, and taketh to him seven other spirits more wicked than himself; and they enter in, and dwell there: and the last state of that man is worse than the first.

Remember we read that Jesus said, Satan's Kingdom is not divided. Therefore we can relate to this Scripture. After the demon(s) is cast out, the man is now ready to be filled with God's Spirit. His body (referred to as his house) is swept and garnished, meaning there is an opening left there. The demon(s) come back and he takes with him seven more spirits more wicked than the himself. That means just one thing; Satan has helpers, a/k/a demons working along with him. Some spirits are more wicked than others. There are spirits of **lust, strife, anger, lying, seditions, adultry** and many more. The demon carried in more demons more wicked than himself and the man was worse off than he was in the first place.

PART IX

A BRIEF REVIEW
OF THE WORKS
OF SATAN

Chapter 30

SATAN BEGUILES EVE - ADAM DID EAT

As we continue, our aim is to show you the force behind the person or the person behind the deed as it was in the Garden of Eden. Let us review the following: Satan entered the serpent and beguiled Eve and she did eat. She gave unto Adam and he did eat and they both sinned before God.

Genesis 3:6-7

And when the woman saw that the tree was good for food, and that it was pleasant to the eyes, and a tree desired to make one wise, she took of the fruit thereof, and did eat; and gave also unto her husband with her; and he did eat. And the eyes of them both were opened, and they knew that they were naked; and they sewed fig leaves together, and made themselves aprons.

THE PUNISHMENT OF CAIN

Cain slew Abel, his brother, God cursed Cain and Cain cried out, "My punishment is greater than I can bear." **(Genesis 4)**

Genesis 4:8-10

And Cain talked with Abel, his brother: and it came to pass, when they were in the field, that Cain rose up against Abel his brother, and slew him. And the Lord said unto Cain, where is Abel thy brother? And he said, I know not:

Am I my brother's keeper? And he said, What hast thou done? The voice of thy brother's blood crieth unto me from the ground."

2ND GENERATION CURSED

Genesis 4:11-13

And now art thou cursed from the earth, which hath opened her mouth to receive thy brother's blood from thy hand; When thou tillest the ground, it shall not henceforth yeild unto thee her strength; a fugitve and a vagabond shalt thou be in the earth. And Cain said unto the Lord, My punishment is greater than I can bear.

We are reminded that sin (the Devil) caused Adam and Eve to be driven from the garden; Cain was wrought because God would not accept his offering. Cain rose up against his brother and slew him. Punishment was upon him and he cries out, *"my punishment is greater that I can bear."* Satan, the motivator, did not tell him what the consequences would be. But, he drove him to this. We see Satan moving and working. His job is to destroy. Again, the word of God has reached its mark.

A PERFECT CREATED BEING

Ezekiel 28th chapter tells us that Satan was perfect in the day he was created, until iniquity was found in him. **Ezekiel 28:3** is referring to Satan.

Behold thy art wiser than Daniel; there is no secret that they can hide from thee:

Remember I said that this is a chapter that many people

184

have a lot of trouble with. Ezekiel 28, starts out with the rebuke of the King of Tyrus. Tyrus was a seaport town where much traffic came in and went out. Therefore, God was rebuking the king of Tyrus. However, we are after the motivator of the King, that is the most important thing. Keep in mind the King of Tyre and who is in back of him.

Son of man, take up a lamentation upon the king of Tyrus, and say unto him, Thus saith the Lord God; Thou sealest up the sum, full of wisdom and perfect in beauty. Thou has been in Eden in the garden of God; every precious stone was thy covering, the sardius, topaz and the diamond, the beryl, the onyx, and the jasper, the sapphire, the emerald, and the carbuncle, and gold: the workmanship of thy tabrets and of thy pipes prepared in thee in the day that thou wast created.

Here we find that God is talking about a created being. Let us continue reading:

Ezekiel 28:14-19
Thou art the anointed cherub that covereth, and I have set thee so; thou wast upon the holy mountain of God; thou has walked up and down in the midst of the stones of fire. Thou was perfect in thy ways from the day that wast created, till inquity was found in thee.

All of the Scriptures we have placed in this book are the word of God showing us Satan behind the deeds being done.

THE WAR IN HEAVEN;
Let us review **Revelation, Chapter 12.** The reason being so many ask the question, "Where did Satan come

from?" Let us start with the seventh verse:

Revelation 12:7-12

And there was war in heaven: Michael and his angels fought against the dragon: and the dragon fought and his angels, And prevailed not; neither was their place found any more in heaven. And the great dragon was cast out, that old serpent, called the Devil, and Satan, which deceiveth the whole world: he was cast out into the earth and his angels were cast out with him. And I heard a loud voice saying in heaven, Now is come salvation, and strength, and the kingdom of our God, and the power of his Christ: for the accuser of our brethren is cast down, which accused them before our God day and night. And they overcame him by the blood of the Lamb, and by the word of their testimony; and they loved not their lives unto the death. Therefore rejoice, ye heavens, and ye that dwell in them. Woe to the inhabiters of the earth and of the sea! for the devil is come down unto you, having great wrath, because he knoweth he hath but a short time.

THE FOREKNOWLEDGE OF GOD

God already knowing this would take place had prepared a Lamb (Jesus) before the foundation of the world to counteract the attack of the evil force that came down to fight and accuse the brethren. **"Satan"** is a Hebrew word signifying adversary, accuser, enemy, most commonly known as Satan or Devil, the chief of the evil spirits.

Some think that Satan will be the one casting souls into hell, however, in these later times he will be the one in hell, who will be cast into the lake of fire and brimstone.

Revelation 20:10

And the devil that deceived them was cast into the lake of

186

fire and brimstone, where the beast and the false prophet are, and shall be tormented day and night for ever and ever.

This is the reason why he is working so hard to destroy and deceive us.

PART X

THE MOTIVATOR
BEHIND THE WORKS
(CONTINUED)

Chapter 31

THE MOTIVATOR CHOKES THE WORD

Let us go from **St. Matthew 16** to **St. Mark 4:13-20**. I will start with this parable at the latter part to show the motivator at work. Verse 14: *"The sower soweth the word."* The Word is Jesus Himself. Many people can sow the word, but the first Word was God. He brought Christ into the world. Apostle Paul stated:

I Corinthians 3:6-7
I have planted, Apollos watered; but God gave the increase. So then neither is he that planteth anything, neither he that watereth; but God that giveth the increase.

The sower is anyone that preaches the gospel, carries the word or tells the word of God. Jesus is speaking to Israel, knowing that they are a pastored people. They were farmers and he taught something that they were familiar with; seeds are something every farmer uses every season. They knew what sowers were, because they sowed wheat, grain, etc. Jesus is speaking to their knowledge that they might understand. Let us read **St. Mark 4** beginning at verse **15:**

Mark 4:15-17
And these are they by the way side, where the word is sown; but when they have heard, Satan cometh immediately, and taketh away the word that was sown in their hearts. And they are they likewise which are sown on

191

stony ground; who, when they have heard the word, immediately receive it with gladness; And have no root in themselves, and so endure but for a time: afterward, when affliction or persecution ariseth for the word's sake, immmediatley they are offended.

Persecution can come through your mother, father, brother, sister, wife, husband, neighbor, children, and people from all walks of life. However, if we know who the motivator is we look at in a different light. Sometimes we think that the person is just angry with us. But Satan has control and he is moving in the person to work evil against us, no matter what it may be. No doubt you have heard people say God told me to do this and when you see their action you know it is not of God.

Let us take at look at **St. Mark 4:18**
And these are they which are sown among thorns; such as hear the word.

There are a lot of thorns when people do their own thing.

St. Mark 4:19:
And the cares of this world, and the deceitfulness of riches, and the lusts of other things entering in, choke the word, and it becometh unfruitful.

You cannot trust in riches or depend on them. *Unfruitfulness*, is the work of Satan. The cares of this world, deceitfulness, riches, and the lust of things enter in and choke the word of God, therefore, the individual becomes unfruitful. Satan is the choker. He is the motivator to cause just that.

....NOT IF IT FALLS ON GOOD GROUND

Let us look at the good ground:

St. Mark 4:20

And these are they which are sown on good ground; such as hear the word, and receive it, and bring forth fruit, some thirtyfold, some sixty, and some an hundred.

Isn't this good news! In other words, those that hear the word, keep the word, and press their way means the word is falling on good ground. And when Satan deceives us we have good ground to stand on. Yes, we have trials and tribulations.

Psalms 34:19.

Many are the afflictions of the righteous, but the Lord deliveth him out of them all.

Romans 8:28:

And we know that all things work together for good to them that love God, to them who are the called according to his purpose.

Romans 8:31, 35-37:

What shall we say then to these things? If God be for us, who can be against us? Who shall separate us from the love of Christ? shall tribulation, or distress, or persecution, or famine, or nakedness, or peril or sword? As it is written, For thy sake we are killed all the day long; we are accounted as sheep for the slaughter. Nay, in all these things we are more than conquerors through him that loved us.

RESIST THE DEVIL AND HE WILL FLEE:

James 4:7
Submit yourselves therefore unto God. Resist the devil and he will flee from you.

Remember the suffering of Job. Job submitted himself unto God and he resisted the Devil. Job resisted even when Satan took away all his possessions, his family and his health. His wife even turned on him. Job passed the test by not charging God foolishly. He was called according to God's purpose because he showed his faith unmovable in the true and living God. We see that Job's riches were taken from him but he did not trust in his riches. This made a big difference. He was not wrapped up in the cares of this world or the lust of this world. Job held on fast to his integrity. Therefore, he was able to endure. Job certainly brought forth thirty, sixty, one hundred fold. I would say that Job brought forth one hundred fold, because when we read our Bible and see the faith of Job and how Job resisted the Devil.

Let us see what Jesus is saying when he spoke about the one that heareth the word and it falls by the wayside.(**St. Mark 4:4**)

St Mark 4:15
And these are they by the wayside, where the word is sown; but when they have heard, Satan cometh immediately, and taketh away the word that was sown in their hearts.

How many times have you told people about the goodness of God, how He saves, etc., and the next time you see those people, you think they have become your adversary and they are working against you. These same individuals seemed willing the very first time but after that they were very unwilling.

You may notice that we are doing a lot of reading. Remember this is a study book. I am giving you enough Scriptures for you to understand what is taking place.

Chapter 32

DEMONS ARE SUBJECT UNTO THE BELIEVERS

St. Luke 10:16-24:

He that heareth you heareth me; and he that despiseth you despiseth me; and he that despiseth me despiseth him that sent me. And the seventy returned again with joy, saying, Lord, even the devils are subject unto us through thy name.

Through the name of Jesus Satan was subject unto the disciples, just as he is unto us today. Therefore, anytime we cast out demons we must do it in the name of Jesus and the authority of Jesus Christ, and it shall be done. These men had not received the Holy Ghost as of yet, but Jesus still gave them power over the Devil. You must read St. Matthew, Chapter 10 as well. It really makes a child of God feel good, however, the Lord lets you know it is not you that casts them out, but Jesus, the word of God.)

St. Luke 10:18

And he said unto them, I beheld Satan as lightning fall from heaven.
(This verse ties in with our lesson because it verifies that Satan came from heaven.)

St. Luke 10:19

Behold, I give you power to tread on serpents and scorpions, and over all power of the enemy: and nothing by any means hurt you.

Serpents and scorpions represent the ways of man. They are serpents and scorpions when they are doing evil, because the Devil is working; evil is the work of devils and demons. Very rarely will you find the learned man or the prudent man casting out demons. You did not find the Pharisees casting out devils because the Devil was motivating them, neither did you find the scribes casting out demons. These were the prudent, the wise.

St. Luke 10:20
Notwithstanding in this rejoice not, that the spirits are subject unto you; but rather rejoice , because your names are written in heaven.

Rejoice because your name is written in heaven. There are many that are not going to rejoice although they have done works in the Lord's name.

St. Matthew 7:21-23
Not every one that saith unto me, Lord, Lord shall enter into the kingdom of heaven; but he that doeth the will of my father which is in heaven. Many will say to me in that day, Lord, Lord, have we not prophesied in thy name? And in thy name have cast out devils? And in thy name done many wonderful works. And then will I profess unto them, I never knew you: depart from me, ye that work iniquity.

Apostle Paul also recognized that if he did not do the will of God, he, too, would be a castaway.

I Corinthians 9:27
But I keep under my body, and bring it into subjection; lest that by any means, when I have preached to others, I

myself should be a castaway.

Therefore rejoice. Let us now see where Jesus rejoiced in his spirit.

St. Luke 10:21

In that hour Jesus rejoiced in his spirit, and said, I thank thee, O Father, Lord of heaven and earth, that thou hast hid these things from the wise and prudent, and hast revealed them unto babes: even so Father; for so it seemed good in thy sight.

The babes were the fishermen, the tax collectors, etc. The man that is really down to earth. He wasn't able to boast and God was able to use these simple people.

St. Luke 10:22-23

All things are delivered to me of my Father: and no man knoweth who the Son is but the Father, and who the Father is, but the Son, and he to whom the Son will reveal him. In that hour Jesus rejoiced in his spirit, and said, I thank thee, O Father, Lord of heaven and earth, that thou has hid these things from the wise and prudent, and hast revealed them unto babes: even so Father: for it seemed good in thy sight. Father; and who the Father is, but the Son, and he to whom the Son will reveal him. And he turned him unto his disciples, and said privately, Blessed are the eyes which see the things that ye see. For I tell you that many prophets and kings have desired to see those things which ye see, and have not seen them; and to hear those things which ye hear, and have not heard them.

In other words the works of Jesus Christ, including the casting out of devils is what they desired to see. We see it because of Pentecost, the dying of our Lord and Savior, and the resurrection on the third day. Grace, the dispensation which we are now living in is a tremendous dispensation. The Bible says the law was given by Moses, but Grace and Truth came by Jesus Christ. Therefore, we see miracles; the casting out of demons, healings of many kinds and people being filled with the Holy Spirit.

Chapter 33

SATAN, AFFLICTION AND INFIRMITY WORKING TOGETHER

St. Luke 13:10-13

And he was teaching in one of the synagogues on the sabbath. And, behold, there was a woman which had a spirit of infirmity eighteen years, and was bowed together, and could in no wise lift up herself. And when Jesus saw her, he called her to him, and said unto her, Woman, thou art loosed from thine infirmity. And he laid his hands on her: and immediately she was made straight, and glorified God.

Satan, the motivator, the spirits of infirmity and affliction had this woman bound. We see how the woman was loosen from these spirits by Jesus speaking the words "loosed" the woman from that spirit in this case, speaking the words, "Woman, thou art loosed." The demonic spirits have ears to hear. Then Jesus laid his hands on the woman and she was made straight (healed.) You would think everyone would be joyous for the woman, but some were not.

St. Luke 13:14-16

And the ruler of the synagogue answered with indignation, because that Jesus had healed on the sabbath day, and said unto the people, There are six days in which man ought to work: in them therefore come and be healed, and not on the sabbath day. The Lord then answered him and said,

Thou hypocrite, doth not each one of you on the sabbath loose his ox or his ass from the stall, and lead him away to the watering? And ought not this woman, being a daughter of Abraham, whom Satan hath bound, lo, these eighteen years, be loosed from this bond on the sabbath day?

Here we observe that Jesus on the Sabbath day loosed the woman who had been bound by Satan, who wants wrap us up and keep us bound in order to destroy us. But Jesus was able to recognize what type of spirit it was that had this woman in the condition she was in, therefore, he was able to lay hands on her and speak the words *"be loosed."*

Chapter 34

SATAN MOTIVATES PETER
TO REBUKE JESUS

Let us take a look at **St. Matthew 16** and observe Jesus talking to his disciples. In this chapter we also find Satan, the Motivator.

St. Matthew 16:20

Then charged he his disciples that they should tell no man that he was Jesus the Christ. From that time forth began Jesus to shew unto his disciples, how that he must go unto Jerusalem, and suffer many things of the elders and chief priests and scribes and be killed, and be raised again the third day. Then Peter took him, and began to rebuke him, saying, Be it far from thee Lord: this shall not be unto thee. But he turned, and said unto Peter Get thee behind me, Satan: thou art an offence unto me: for thou savourest not the things that be of God, but those that be of men.

This may seem a little hard, but nevertheless, it is true. Here Jesus is showing them the things that will take place in His life. Knowing very well for this purpose He had come into the world to give His life for your sins and mine. In other words, Jesus came to cover Adam's sins; to blot out the handwriting and ordinances against us, as it is written by the Apostle Paul in *So then why wasn't adam saved too?*

Colossians 2:14.

Blotting out the handwriting of ordinances that was against

203

us, which was contrary to us, and took it out of the way, nailing it to his cross:

This is what Jesus Christ was showing to his disciples, however, if you notice that Peter rebuked Him saying, these things shall not be. Jesus looked past Peter, at the motivator himself and He was able to recognize him. This is where we come short so many times. We are not able to recognize the motivator. Jesus said, "Get thee behind me, Satan. Thou art an offense to me." Satan is an offense to Jesus! He is an adversary, against Christ, and he is the Anti-Christ. Therefore, Jesus, by passing Peter speaks directly to the Devil. We do that today. At times we hear a person speaking that which is contrary and we know it is the Devil. If you were to say that to the individual, the person would probably get very angry and say, "Why are you talking to me like that? Who do you think you are?" However, if all of us were able to recognize the Devil when he speaks and if all of us would say the same thing, I am sure we would get accustomed to it and I am quite sure we would watch more closely what we say.

Jesus knew that the Devil was speaking when Peter denied that this thing would come to pass, however, we find Jesus discerning the spirits.

Chapter 35

SATAN MOTIVATES JUDAS ISCARIOT

St. John 13:21-32:

When Jesus had thus said, he was troubled in spirit, and testified, and said, Verily, verily, I say unto you, that one of you shall betray me. Then the disciples looked one on another, doubting of whom he spake. Now there was leaning on Jesus' bosom one of his disciples, whom Jesus loved. Simon Peter therefore beckoned to him, that he should ask who it should be of whom he spake. He then lying on Jesus' breast saith unto him, Lord, who is it? Jesus answered, He it is, to whom I shall give a sop, when I have dipped it. And when he had dipped the sop, he gave it to Judas Iscariot, the son of Simon. And after the sop Satan entered into him. Then Jesus said unto him, That thou doest, do quickly. Now no man at the table knew for what intent he spake this unto him. For some of them thought, because Judas had the bag, that Jesus had said unto him, Buy those things that we have need of against the feast; or that he should give something to the poor. He then having received the sop went immediately out; and it was night. Therefore, when he was gone out, Jesus said, Now is the Son of man glorified, and God is glorified in him. If God be glorified in him, God shall also glorify him in himself, and shall straightway glorify him.

When Satan entered into the heart of Judas, he set right out to betray Jesus. Jesus knew very well that it was Judas that would betray him. Judas carried the money bag all the time that he went in and out with Jesus. Yet, he was a thief and Jesus knew it. Let us look a the word of God and see what happened unto Judas.

St. Matthew 27:3-5

Then Judas, which had betrayed him, when he saw that he was condemned, repented himself, and brought again the thirty pieces of silver to the chief priests and elders, Saying, I have sinned in that I have betrayed innocent blood. And they said, What is that to us? see thou to that. And he cast down the pieces of silver in the temple, and departed, and went and hanged himself.

Judas opened up, Satan walked right in and the act of betrayal was committed. The Bible lets us know that after Judas had betrayed Jesus, he thought that they would admonish him or scourge him a little bit and let him go. However, Judas found out that they wanted to put Jesus to death. When Judas found this out, he said, *"I have sinned in that I have betrayed innocent blood."* Judas knew that Jesus had done no wrong, but he was greedy, and greed blinded him. Satan entered into the heart of Judas and blinded him. This is the reason Judas was able to covenant with them for thirty pieces of silver. Judas sold our Lord. The same Devil that deceived him did not tell him what would happen to him after. Judas committed suicide. We have many that are saying that if you commit suicide, you can be saved. This is a lie of the Devil. Satan is deceiving because God's word says:

Exodus 20:13
Thou shalt not kill.

When an individual takes his own life, how can he ask for forgiveness? He will be lost to eternal damnation. The Bible says to break one commandment is to break the whole law. When we kill, we take a life and that is murder.

... for giving me ... by ... in which ...
Bill was the great-grandfather ... his brother ...
... when we killed ... life and that afternoon.

Chapter 36

SATAN DESIRES TO SIFT PETER

St. Luke 22:31-34:

And the Lord said, Simon, Simon, behold, Satan hath desired to have you, that he may sift you as wheat: But I have prayed for thee, that thy faith fail not: and when thou art converted, strengthen thy brethren. (On the day of Pentecost, Peter received the Holy Ghost with power. This was the conversion Jesus was speaking about.) *And he said unto him, Lord, I am ready to go with thee, both into prison and to death. And he said, I tell thee, Peter, the cock shall not crow this day, before that thou shalt thrice deny that thou knowest me.*

Jesus is speaking to Peter, knowing, very well, that Peter had a desire to please him. This can happen to all of us. but Jesus knew the heart of Peter. Peter had good desires and he loved Jesus, but Peter had weaknesses. He was quick to speak, and later he denied Jesus, however, Jesus knew that Peter possessed a good desire. His desire was go to prison with him, even die with him. Jesus told Peter, "Before the cock crow twice, thy shalt deny me thrice," and the deed took place. You see here Satan was very much on the job and he did his job well. We realize that all this took place before Pentecost. This was the unconverted Peter. Notice that Jesus said

St. Luke 22:32.

...and *when thou art converted, strengthen thy brethren.*

209

Why would Jesus say, "when thou art converted?" Peter was a man that was walking with Christ and casting out devils. He came back with the others rejoicing, saying, even the spirits are subject unto us.

THE CONVERSION

This was the unconverted Peter that Jesus said would deny him thrice, however, on the day of Pentecost Peter was converted. Many times we take the word **"converted"** very lightly. People in churches have a way of being converted. Some feel conversion comes when they have shaken the preacher's hand; others feel conversion is putting their names on the church roll. These are not conversions. The true conversion came on the day of Pentecost.

Acts 2:1-4

And when the day of Pentecost was fully come, they were all with one accord in one place. And suddenly there came a sound from heaven as of a rushing mighty wind, and it filled all the house where they were sitting. And there appeared unto them cloven tongues like as of fire, and it sat upon each of them. And they were all filled with the Holy Ghost, and began to speak with other tongues, as the Spirit gave them utterance.

This is the good news. It was the Spirit that gave them utterance. This was Peter's conversion. When Apostle Peter came out of the upper room, he came preaching that Christ is the son of God.

Acts 2:14-21

But, Peter, standing up with the eleven, lifted up his voice, and said unto them, Ye men of Judea, and all ye that dwell at Jerusalem, be this known unto you, and hearken to my words. For these are not drunken as ye suppose, seeing it is but the third hour of the day. But this is that which was spoken by the prophet Joel; And it shall come to pass in the last days, saith God, I will pour out my Spirit upon all flesh: and your sons and daughters shall prophesy, and your young men shall see visions, and your old men shall dream dreams: And on my servants and on thy hand-maidens I will pour out in those days of my Spirit; and they shall prophesy. And I will shew wonders in heaven above, and signs in the earth beneath; blood, and fire, and vapour of smoke. The sun shall be turned into darkness, and the moon into blood, before that great and notable day of the Lord come. And is shall come to pass, that whosoever shall call on the name of Lord shall be saved.

After Pentecost, although Apostle Peter was a strong man, weaknesses in Peter still showed up: Let us look at a situation where Apostle Paul had to rebuke Apostle Peter for weakness in his character.

There was a time, according to the scripture, when certain brethren would show up from Jerusalem, Peter would be eating with the Gentiles. When the Jews would come, Peter would turn away from the Gentiles. Even Barnabas was carried away with this dissimulation. Apostle Paul had to rebuke Apostle Peter.

Galatians 2:11-14
But when Peter was come to Antioch, I withstood him to the face, because he was to be blamed. For before that certain came from James, he did eat with the Gentiles: but when they were come, he withdrew and separated himself, fearing them which were of the circumcision. And the other

211

Jews dissembled likewise with him; insomuch that Barnabas was also carried away with their dissimulation. But when I saw that the walked not uprightly according to the truth of the gospel, I said unto Peter before them all, If thou, being a Jew, livest after the manner of Gentiles, and not as do the Jews, why compellest thou the Gentiles to live as do the Jews.

After Apostle Peter's conversion, he stood for Jesus Christ all the way and was martyred in the city of Rome.

Chapter 37

SATAN, THE MOTIVATOR, ANANIAS AND SAPPHIRA

The book of **Acts, Chapter 5** records some of the things that took place after the resurrection of Jesus Christ. It is quite lengthy, but we are not going into all of it, however, this portion of Scripture will give us another account of the works of Satan, the Motivator.

ACTS 5:1-11

But a certain man named Ananias, with Sapphira, his wife, sold a possession. And kept back part of the price, his wife also being privy to it, and brought a certain part and laid it at the apostles' feet. But Peter said, Ananias, why hath Satan filled thine heart to lie to the Holy Ghost, and to keep back part of the price of the land? Whiles it remained, was it not thine own? and after it was sold, was it not in thine own power? why hast thou conceived this thing in thine heart? thou has not lied unto men, but unto God. And Ananias hearing these words fell down, and gave up the ghost: and great fear came on all them that heard these things. And the young men arose, wound him up, and carried him out, and buried him. And it was about the space of three hours after, when his wife, not knowing what was done, came in. And Peter answered unto her, Tell me whether ye sold the land for so much? And she said, Yea, for so much. Then Peter said unto her, How is it that ye have agreed together to tempt the Spirit of the Lord?

behold, the feet of them which have buried thy husband are at the door, and shall carry thee out. Then fell she down straightway at his feet, and yielded up the ghost: and the young men came in, and found her dead, and, carrying her forth, buried her by her husband. And great fear came upon all the church, and upon as many as heard these things.

Here we see a battle between God and Satan. Satan, The Motivator, put this into Ananias heart: sell your goods, pretend you are in agreement with everyone else, come and lay your goods at the Apostle's feet, act as if you are 100% for the church and willing to sacrifice for the word of God's sake. Ananias and Sapphira were hypocrites. Satan motivated Ananias and Sapphira to lie unto Peter and they were convinced that they would get away with it. When they came and spoke to Peter, they found a man full of the Holy Ghost who was able to discern that it was the Devil on the job motivating. Apostle Peter recognized what Spirit it was that caused them to do this evil. He even told them when you had the land it belonged to you, therefore, you did not have to lie about it. You could have come in and spoken the truth. But this is the way Satan works. His job is to try to get us to exaggerate to the extreme, making it a lie. No exaggeration is part of the truth because a lie is a lie! Remember the word of God says Satan was a murderer and liar from the beginning.

St. John 8:44:

Ye are of your father the devil, and the lusts of your father ye will do. He was a murderer from the beginning, and abode not in the truth, because there is no truth in him. When he speaketh a lie, he speaketh of his own: for he is a liar, and the father of it. And because I tell you the truth, ye believe me not.

Chapter 38

SATAN MOTIVATES
FORNICATION AND INCEST

I Corinthians 5:1-13:

It is reported commonly that there is fornication among you, and such fornication as is not so much as named among the Gentiles, that one should have his father's wife. And ye are puffed up, and have not rather mourned, that he that hath done this deed might be taken away from among you. For I verily, as absent in body, but present in spirit, have judged already, as though I were present, concerning him that hath so done this deed. In the name of our Lord Jesus Christ, when ye are gathered together, and my spirit, with the power of our Lord Jesus Christ, To deliver such an one unto Satan for the destruction of the flesh, that the spirit may saved in the day of the Lord Jesus. Your glorying is not good. Know ye not that a little leaven leaventh the whole lump? Purge out therefore the old leaven, that ye may be a new lump, as ye are unleavened. For even Christ our passover is sacrificed for us: Therefore let us keep the feast, not with the old leaven, neither with the leaven of malice and wickedness; but with the unleavened bread of sincerity and truth. I wrote unto you in an epistle not to company with fornicators: Yet not altogether with the fornicators of this world, or with the covetous, or extortioners, or with idolators; for then must ye needs go out of the world. But now I have written unto you not to keep company, if any man that is called a brother be a fornicator, or covetous, or an idolator, or a railer, or a drunkard, or an extortioner; with such an one no not to eat. For what have I to do to judge them also that are without? do not ye judge them that are within? But them that are without God judgeth. Therefore put away from among yourselves that wicked person.

Here, again is the Apostle Paul speaking to the church at Corinth. Satan motivated the man to lay with his father's wife. The church knew that this act was committed and instead of moaning or being sorrowful, and praying to God and asking God for deliverance, they were puffed up. This is exactly what the Devil will do, seeing that he is a spirit of Pride. His fall from heaven came about because of that spirit of Pride. He was lifted up in his own beauty.

AFTER LUST IS CONCEIVED

After the act of fornication was done, the man, the church refused to go back and ask God for forgiveness. The church put up with it and they went about their own business as if nothing happened. This is what the Devil wanted in the first place. He motivated that person and he caused him to fall from the grace of God and caused the church to be in a puffed up state. Apostle Paul informed the church, that although I be absent in body I am going to judge this matter. Since the man was serving the Devil, Apostle Paul gave him over to the Devil for the destruction of his flesh. This is what the Devil wanted. By the man's actions he was serving Satan. Now the Devil could destroy his flesh, that his spirit might be saved in the day of the Lord. This was a mercy killing. To make it plain would be to say, if this man is this way, he will do it again and again because Satan is at work. When you opened up these spirits will come in. What Apostle Paul is saying to do is to turn

218

him over. He is not saying "once in Christ, never out", as a lot of people are saying today. We can break that seal of God. We can go so far out that our soul will not be saved 0n the day of the Lord. Apostle Paul stated: *"Know ye not that a little leaven leaventh the whole lump."* In other words, don't hang out with folks doing the Devil's work.

Chapter 39

SATAN MOTIVATES ADULTERY

I Corinthians 7:1-5:

Now concerning the things whereof ye wrote unto me: It is good for a man not to touch a woman. Nevertheless, to avoid fornication, let every man have his own wife, and let every woman have her own husband. Let the husband render unto the wife due benevolence: and likewise also the wife unto the husband. The wife hath not power of her own body, but the husband: and likewise also the husband hath not power of his own body, but the wife. Defraud ye not one the other, except it be with consent for a time, that ye may give yourselves to fasting and prayer; and come together again, that Satan tempt you not for your incontinency.

Here we find Apostle Paul saying that the Devil wants to motivate or trick the husband and/or his wife to commit adultery, therefore, he is saying if you separate for a period of time do it with consent because Satan can creep in there and you will find yourself with another problem. In other words Satan will be the master at that time.

Chapter 40

SATAN MOTIVATES UNFORGIVENESS

II Corinthians 2:9-10:

For to this end also did I write, that I might know the proof of you, whether ye be obedient in all things. To whom ye forgive any thing, I forgive also: for if I forgave anything, to whom I forgave it, for your sakes forgave I it in the person of Christ; Lest Satan should get an advantage of us: for we are not ignorant of his devices.

Apostle Paul is letting us to know not to be uniformed about the devices or methods of the Devil, because it is very important to forgive. The most important thing in our spiritual life is to learn how to forgive one another. Let us read the words of Jesus Christ:

St. Matthew 6:14-15:

For if ye forgive men their trespasses, your heavenly Father will also forgive you: But if ye forgive not men their trespasses, neither will your Father forgive your trespasses.

If we do not forgive that neighbor or whoever that person may be, God will not forgive us. The Apostle Peter said unto Jesus:

St. Matthew 18:21-22

Lord, how oft shall my brother sin against me, and I forgive him? till seven times? Jesus saith unto him, I say not unto

223

thee, Until seven times: but, Until seventy times seventy.

In other words, it will be so many times you will not be able to count. Just as Apostle Paul says that he is not ignorant of Satan's devices, I would to God that we could all say the same identical thing and hold to it and not just say it in words, but be able to carry it out. Remember we are not ignorant.

Chapter 41

TRANSFORMED INTO
AN ANGEL OF LIGHT

II Corinthians 11:13:

For such are false apostles, deceitful workers, trans-forming themselves into the apostles of Christ. And no marvel; for Satan himself is transformed into an angel of light. Therefore it is no great thing if his ministers also be transformed as the ministers of righteousness; whose end shall be according to their works.

Apostles Paul is warning us about the deceitful workers and false apostles leading the people astray. We have a lot of them out there today. They are not Christ's disciples, but deceitful workers. This is why Apostle Paul stated in the 14th verse that Satan can bring you something and you will think it is of God. This is a tragedy among God's people. Their theme song is 'God told me this...'Many times God has not told them anything. We have many people prophesying falsely. They say it is the Spirit of God, but it is just the flesh. It is Satan that motivates many times. I want you to understand I am not against prophecy. I am one hundred percent for prophecy. It is one of the most important gifts in our churches, but the saints tend to use it so loosely. They say the Lord told me this and the Lord told me that and the next day they have forgotten about what the Lord told them and they are doing just the opposite. Satan loves this gift because he loves to operate it himself. He is doing a tremendous job and many people believe him. This is one of the reasons he can come in and present himself as one coming to enlighten people to God's will. In other words to let you know what God's will is for you. However, what Satan is actually doing is trying to destroy the church, your credibility and to get everyone to believe a lie, because, as Jesus says, he is the father of lies.

THE FATHER OF LIES

St. John 8:44:
Ye are of your father the devil, and the lusts of your father ye will do. He was a murderer from the beginning, and abode not in the truth, because there is no truth in him. When he speaketh a lie, he speaketh of his own: for he is a liar, and the father of it. And because I tell you the truth, ye believe me not.

Therefore, when people come and say God told me to tell you this or that, I am very careful and watchful. In all of my years in the ministry, I have not found God to be a blabbermouth. He gives us the Bible full of His word and He does not put us into everyone's business either. I can use myself as an example. I have had many visions, revelations and many words from the Lord. Therefore I weigh very carefully what people say to me. The first thing I do, is to find out if it is according to (Bible) the word of God. The word of God must back it up. Satan can change one word. Remember God told Adam, the day ye eat thereof ye shall surely die. Satan said, *"ye shall not surely die"* (Genesis 3:4). Sometimes a word will come to us so strongly, that the Spirit of God will rise up in you. What is actually happening it that the Spirit of God is discerning and rejecting that spirit talking to you and you think the Spirit is rising up in you to speak what you hear. However, it is just the opposite. The Holy Spirit is saying, **"Don't speak, it is Satan himself."** Many times the saints say "I felt so good in the spirit, I just went on and said it." This is the danger. The church has got to watch that feeling good in the spirit, because this is not a feeling thing but a knowing thing. It is important to know and to discern.

Chapter 42

SATAN, THE MOTIVATOR,
THE THORN IN THE FLESH

II Corinthians 12:1-3:
It is not expedient for me doubtless to glory, I will come to visions and revelations of the Lord. I knew a man in Christ above fourteen years ago, (whether in the body, I cannot tell; or whether out of the body, I cannot tell God knoweth:) such an one caught up to the third heaven. And I knew such a man, (whether in the body, or out of the body, I cannot tell: God knoweth;)

Here we find Apostle Paul was caught up in the Spirit. It was so real, he did not know whether he had his flesh on or not.

GOD'S GRACE IS SUFFICIENT
All through these persecutions, infirmities and trials that Satan put Apostle Paul through, these are the things that he would glory in. Many times Satan will draw us closer to Christ, whether we know it or not. When the Devil drives us into the arms of God it is then that we fast and pray. When Satan put the pressure on Apostle Paul, God's answer to him was:

II Corinthians 12:9
My grace is sufficient for thee: for my strength is made perfect in weakness.

In other words, God is saying, I am not going to move it, but my grace will see you through. God gives us enough strength to bear it. Sometimes we think that we are at the end of the rope and we cannot go any further. I have witnessed this many times in my ministry. I felt like I could not go on any further. But everytime God brings me right through and I go on to something higher (man extremities are God's opportunities) This is how God strengthens us. Jesus told Satan:

St. Matthew 4:10

Get thee hence Satan: for it is written, Thou shalt worship the Lord thy God, and him only shall thy serve.

When Jesus said "thou," he meant Satan. You are the servant of God and Him only shall you serve. God allows Satan to work, and He will stop him when He gets ready to stop him. He'll allow him to go but so far. Remember God allowed Satan to touch Job's body and everything he had, but He did not allow him to take his life. Unto Satan, God said:

Job 2:6

And the Lord said unto Satan, Behold he is in thine hand; but save his life.

Remember Satan, the Motivator, can only motivate as much as God will allow him to.

PART XI

THE STUDY OF
THE HOLY SPIRIT

Chapter 43

THE HOLY SPIRIT

The portion of this manual is set aside for the teaching on the Holy Spirit. The Holy Spirit is very controversial, even today. We are living in a time when people are denying the power of the Holy Ghost. He is the power of God. I would like to begin with the book of beginnings (**Genesis**) and show the movement of the Holy Spirit. However, before we go there, let us read a portion of Jesus' warning unto those who should speak evil of the Holy Spirit. He made it plain in the Scriptures as to the power and the authority of the Holy Spirit and how we should look upon him. Let us first go the gospel according to **St. Matthew**. We will then go back to the book of **Genesis**.

THE UNPARDONABLE SIN
(Blasphemy Against the Holy Spirit)

St. Matthew 12:31-32.

Wherefore I say unto you, All manner of sin and blasphemy shall be forgiven unto men: but the blasphemy against the Holy Ghost shall not be forgiven unto men. And whosoever speaketh a word against the son of man, it shall be forgiven him: but whosoever speaketh against the Holy Ghost, it shall not be forgiven him, neither in this world, neither in the world to come.

Now you see that we dealing with a very serious study.

We must not speak evil against the Holy Ghost. Blasphemy means to contribute the movement of the Holy Spirit and the power of the Holy Spirit to the Devil. This is common among the people today. Some see God put his spirit in people and they speak in tongues and right away it is attributed to the Devil. We must be very careful. This happens even in our churches today, when we see one baptized with the Holy Spirit. Many of us, after we see this thing will say, if he did not receive the Holy Spirit as we received it, then it is of the Devil. Some will even say, you have to fall a certain way. If you fall on the floor or on your back it is the Devil. However, when we attribute God's work to the Devil we are speaking evil against the Holy Ghost. Therefore, I want you to approach this subject very intelligently in order that you might be blessed of God from this study as I continue to broaden your mind and your vocabulary within this Biblical knowledge. Remember we are going to follow the movement of the Holy Spirit throughout the Bible.

Chapter 44

THE MOVEMENT OF THE HOLY SPIRIT

IN THE BEGINNING
Genesis 1:1:
In the beginning God created the heaven and the earth. And the earth was without form and void; and darkness was upon the face of the deep. And the Spirit of God moved upon the face of the water.

The Spirit of God moving upon the face of the water is the Holy Spirit working and moving in the beginning of the creation. This trend of the moving and the working of the Holy Spirit, (God's spirit) is what we are going to follow right through the Bible.

THE HOLY SPIRIT MOVED UPON THE MEN OF THE OLD TESTAMENT.
As we are going through the Bible we will see that the Holy Spirit not only moved upon the face of the deep, but from time to time the Holy Spirit moved upon men in the Old Testament.

MOSES
Moses was full of the Holy Spirit. God took of His Spirit upon Moses and put it upon the seventy elders and they prophesied.

Numbers 11:24-25

And Moses went out, and told the people the words of the Lord, and gathered the seventy men of the elders of the people, and set them round about the tabernacle. And the Lord came down in a cloud, and spake unto him, and took of the spirit that was upon him, and gave it unto the seventy elders: and it came to pass, that, when the spirit rested upon them, they prophesied and they did not cease.

Moses being a Holy man full of the Holy Ghost, was prepared by God to lead his people. He was able to go up to the mountain of God on behalf of his people.

Exodus 20:18-19:

"And all the people saw the thunderings, and the lightnings and the noise of the trumpet, and the mountain smoking: and when the people saw it, they removed, and stood afar off. And they said unto Moses, Speak thou with us, and we will hear: but let not God speak with us, lest we die."

The children of Israel witnessed the thundering and the lightning, and the mountain smoking and they were not able to go up to the Mount of God as was Moses. The same thing is for today. The sinner has no right to go before God, unless he goes confessing. The sinner cannot say "Our Father," unless he has been born again. The Lord's prayer is for us who know the Lord. If we are not doing His will or serving God, how can we say "Our Father." This is why the word says in:

St. John 3:7.
Ye must be born again.

We worship, sing and pray in the Spirit because God is Spirit. Everything we do regarding God, must be done in the Spirit.

St. John 4:24.
God is a Spirit: and they that worship him must worship him in spirit and in truth.

The word of God tells how Moses laid his hand upon Joshua and the spirit of wisdom came upon Joshua.

JOSHUA
Deuteronomy 34:9
And Joshua the son of Nun was full of the spirit of wisdom; for Moses had laid his hands upon him: and the children of Israel hearkened unto him and did as the Lord commanded Moses.

God promised to be with Joshua as He was with His servant Moses.

Joshua 1:1-3
Now after the death of Moses the servant of the Lord it came to pass, that the Lord spake unto Joshua the son of Nun, Moses' minister saying, Moses my servant is dead; now therefore arise, go over this Jordan, thou, and all this people, unto the land which I do give to them, even to the children of Israel. Every place that the sole of your foot shall tread upon, that have I given unto you, as I said unto Moses.

SAMSON
Most of us have read or heard of the story Samson and Delilah. Samson was separated unto God from birth. He was a deliver, anointed by God to deliver His people out of the hands of the Philistines.

Judges 13:3-5.

And the angel of the Lord appeared unto the woman, and said unto her, Behold, now, thou art barren, and bearest not: but thou shalt conceive, and bear a son. Now therefore beware, I pray thee, and drink not wine nor strong drink, and eat not any unclean thing: For, lo, thou shalt conceive, and bear a son; and no razor shall come on his head: for the child shall be a Nazarite unto God from the womb: and he shall begin to deliver Israel out of the hand of the Philistines.

The Spirit of the Lord (Holy Spirit) moved upon Samson on many different occasions that he might fulfill God's will to deliver his people. Here are just a few instances.

Judges 13:24-25; 14:5-6.

And the woman bare a son, and called his name Samson: and the child grew, and the Lord blessed him. And the Spirit of the Lord began to move him at times in the camp of Dan between Zorah and Eshtaol. Then Samson went down, and his father and his mother, to Timnath, and came to the vineyards Timnath: and behold, a young lion roared against him. And the Spirit of the Lord came mightily upon him, and he rent a kid, and he had nothing in his hand: but he told not his father or his mother what he had done."

The Bible also shows us how Samson got out of the will of God and the Spirit of the Lord departed from him.

Judges 16:20

And she (Delilah) said, The Philistines be upon thee, Samson. And he awoke out of his sleep, and said, I will go

238

out as at other times before, and shake myself. And he wist
not that he Lord was departed from him.

DANIEL
Daniel 5:11-12.
The word of God says that Daniel had an excellent
spirit in him. That excellent spirit is the Holy Ghost.
There is a man in thy kingdom, in whom is the spirit of the
holy gods; and in the days of thy father light and
understanding and wisdom, like the wisdom of the gods,
was found in him; whom the king Nebuchadnezzar thy
father made master of the magicians, astrologers,
Chaldeans, and Soothsayers. Forasmuch as an excellent
spirit, and knowledge, and understanding, interpreting of
dreams, and shewing of hard sentences, and dissolving of
doubts were found in the same Daniel.

SAUL
Saul was the anointed king over Israel. The Spirit of
God was upon Saul and Saul did prophesy:

I Samuel 10:10.
...and the Spirit of God came upon him, and he prophesied
among them."

JEPHTHAH
The Bible also informs us of the Spirit of God coming
upon Jephthah when he led God's people to victory.

Judges 11:29, 32.
Then the Spirit of the Lord came upon Jephthah...So
Jephthah passed over unto the children of Ammon to fight
against them; and the Lord delivered them into his hands.

ISAIAH
THE SPIRIT OF BURNING

Our next Scripture is **Isaiah 4:4:**
When the Lord shall have washed away the filth of the daughters of Zion, and shall have purged the blood of Jerusalem from the midst thereof by the spirit of judgment, and by the spirit of burning.

God is going to do this by his Spirit. You may ask, how can that be?
Hebrews 12:29
For our God is a consuming fire.

John the Baptist said:
St. Matthew 3:11
...He (Jesus) shall baptize you with the Holy Ghost and fire.

The "*spirit of burning*" that will purify and cleanse is the Holy Spirit. We can see this in the way that God dealt with Isaiah:
Let us look at the beginning of the calling of Isaiah.

Isaiah 6:1:5
In the year that King Uzziah died I saw also the Lord sitting upon a throne, high and lifted up, and his train filled the temple. Above it stood the seraphims: each one had six wings; with twain he covered his face and with twain he covered his feet and with twain he did fly. And one cried unto another, and said, Holy, holy, holy, is the Lord of hosts: the whole earth is full of his glory. And the posts of the door moved at the voice of him that cried, and the house was filled with smoke. Then said I, Woe is me! For

240

I am undone; because I am a man of unclean lips; and I dwell in the midst of a people of unclean lips: for mine eyes have seen the King, the Lord of hosts.

At this point we want to get one main thing correct regarding this Scripture, it is the time of Isaiah's calling. Many preachers, teachers, theologians and so-called Bible scholars and others say that Uzziah had to get out of Isaiah's way so that Isaiah could see God. That is not so. Isaiah is simply identifying the time of his calling. *"In the year king Uzziah died, I saw also the Lord."* Many times we find ourselves referring to different times in our lives by an event that has taken place. For example, you may ask the question, "Do you remember the year of the earthquake, or the big rain or the year when Mrs. Brown died? It was the same year I graduated or I got married or when I was in the hospital. When President Kennedy got shot, I know exactly where I was, and what I was doing, and I might refer to that from time to time. It was a pronounced event that had happened. This is just what Isaiah was doing. King Uzziah was not blocking his way nor standing in his way. I am quite sure that every Jew knew when he died, therefore, Isaiah picked a very substantial fact and time to identify the year that God revealed himself unto him.

After he had seen all of this Isaiah realized just how undone he was. He referred to his unclean lips, meaning he had not the Holy Spirit and the people he dealt with had not the Holy Spirit.

HE IS A CLEANSER: HE IS A PURIFIER: HE PURGES SINS

The Holy Spirit is a cleanser. That is why John said:

St. Matthew 3:11

He [Jesus] *shall baptize you with the Holy Ghost and with fire.*

The Fire is a purifier.

Revelation 3:18.

I counsel thee to buy of me gold tried in the fire.

Gold is purified by putting it through the fire. When it melts and runs like water, I guarantee you that every thing in that gold that is not gold will be burnt up.

Isaiah 6:6

Then flew one of the seraphims unto me, having a live coal in his hand, which he had taken with the tongs from off the altar: And he laid it upon my mouth, and said, Lo, this hath touched thy lips; and thine iniquity is taken away, and thy sin purged. Also I heard the voice of the Lord saying, Whom shall I send, and who will go for us? Then said I; Here am I: send me.

The iniquity is the wrong doing and the sin that was in Isaiah's life which was taken away. Isaiah was referring to the non-righteousness of himself and of Israel, when he cried out, *"I am undone; because I am a man of unclean lips; and I dwell in the midst of a people of unclean lips:"* Israel was a sinful people who did not keep God's law. Isaiah was purged by the live coal. This was the work of the Holy Spirit, cleansing his tongue that he might speak as an oracle of God. After the live coals was placed upon his lips, his sins purged, then Isaiah could say: *"Here am I; send me."*

When God sends us he anoints our mouth to be a

242

spokesman for him. Apostle Paul wrote these words:

Romans 10:14-15
...and how shall they hear without a preacher and how shall he preach, except he be sent.

EZEKIEL

Just as God was now ready to use Isaiah, so it was with Ezekiel. God dealt with him and put him in the Spirit. Let us read:

Ezekiel 2:2
And the spirit entered into me when spake unto me, and set me upon my feet, that I heard him that spake unto me.

Ezekiel 3:14
So the Spirit lifted me, and took me away, and I went in bitterness, in the heat of my spirit; but the hand of the Lord was strong upon me.

Through the Holy Spirit, God showed Ezekiel many spiritual truths. Ezekiel and these other men I have written about represent just a few of the movements of the Spirit in the Old Testament. Remember the Holy Spirit was striving with man, giving man the ability to accomplish God's will. Keep in mind, that we are now living in the (sixth) dispensation of Grace when the Holy Spirit (power of God) will be in you.

Chapter 45

THE HOLY SPIRIT IN YOU

This is why Jesus said unto his disciples,. The spirit will be with you and shall be in you.

St. John 14:17.
Even the Spirit of truth; [Holy Spirit] whom the world cannot receive because it seeth him not, neither knoweth him: but ye know him: for he dwelleth with you and shall be in you.

Humanity likes to say, "Yes, I believe in the Father, Son and the Holy Ghost." I agree, that most people believe in the Father, Son and the Holy Ghost, but we all need to understand the great power that the Holy Spirit has. He guides our lives and He introduces to us the will of God. He is God.

THE PROMISE OF THE OUTPOURING OF THE HOLY SPIRIT

Joel 2:28:
And it shall come to pass afterward, that I will pour out my spirit upon all flesh...

The Spirit of God pouring out upon all flesh is none other than the Holy Spirit. Joel's prophecy came to pass on the day of Pentecost.

PROPHECY FULFILLED - THE DAY OF PENTECOST

Acts 2:1-4

And when the day of Pentecost was fully come, they were all with one accord in one place. And suddenly there came a sound from heaven as of a rushing mighty wind, and it filled all the house where they were sitting. And there appeared unto them cloven tongues like as of fire, and it sat upon each of them. And they were all filled with the Holy Ghost as the Spirit gave utterance.

The multitude, thought surely that these men were drunk with new wine They were not drunk with new wine, they were filled with the Holy Ghost.

Acts 2:6-8, 12-13.

And there were dwelling at Jerusalem Jews, devout men, out of every nation under heaven. Now when this was noised abroad, the multitude came together, and were confounded, because that every man heard them speak in his own language. And they were all amazed, and marvelled, saying to one another, Behold, are not all these which speak Galileans? And how hear we every man in our own tongue, wherein we were born? And they were all amazed, and were in doubt, saying, saying one to another, What meaneth this? Others mocking said, These men are full of new wine.

Chapter 46

THE HOLY SPIRIT VS. THE WATER BAPTISM

At this time, I am going to just touch on the water baptism due to the fact that I have dwelt more extensively with the water baptism in the chapter on The Ministry of John The Baptist. Let us go to St. Matthew 3rd chapter and begin at the 11th verse:

St. Matthew 3:11

I indeed baptize you with water unto repentance: but he that cometh after me is mightier that I, whose shoes I am not worthy to bear: he shall baptize you with the Holy Ghost, and with fire.

This is pertaining to the ministry of John the Baptist and how he was baptizing in the river of Jordan. Men came to be baptized of him confessing their sins. John the Baptist had a great testimony. It is very important that we know and keep in mind the ministry of John the Baptist. So many times people lose sight of the gospel that John preached. The gospel in the sense that this is the word of God being spoken. John said He, meaning Jesus, shall baptize you with the Holy Ghost and fire. John baptized with water. Now most of us know about the water baptism because we received it at one time or another. Some people sprinkle, others submerge, nevertheless, our subject matter we are dealing right now is the baptism of the Holy Spirit. As I have stated, we will go further into the study of the water baptism in the chapter on "The Ministry of John The Baptist." Let us continue reading from St. Matthew 3rd chapter.

St. Matthew 3:12-17

Whose fan is in his hand, and he will throughly purge his floor, and gather his wheat into the garner; but he will burn up the chaff with unquenchable fire. Then cometh Jesus from Galilee to Jordan unto John, to be baptized of him. But John forbad him, saying, I have need to be baptized of thee, and comest thou to me? And Jesus answering said unto him, Suffer it to be so now for thus it becometh us to fulfill all righteousness. Then he suffered him. And Jesus when he was baptized when up straightway out of the water: and lo, the heavens were opened unto him, and he saw the Spirit of God descending like a dove, and lighting upon him: And, lo, a voice from heaven, saying, This is my beloved Son, in whom I am well pleased.

PART XII

THE WORKS OF

THE HOLY SPIRIT

Chapter 47

THE HOLY SPIRIT SPEAKS
ON YOUR BEHALF

St. Mark 13:11-12.

But when they shall lead you an deliver you up, take no thought beforehand what ye shall speak, neither do ye premeditate: but whatsoever shall be given you in that hour, that speak ye: for it is not ye that speak, but the Holy Ghost. Now the brother shall betray the brother to death, and the father the son; and children shall rise up against their parents and shall cause them to be put to death.

What does the Lord mean by this saying, *"when they shall deliver you up....?"* Many times when we have problems we go get a lawyer to take care of the circumstances. However, the Lord is saying that he will be your lawyer, if you go before the judge. This promise is to the individual(s) who have received the Holy Spirit and has surrendered his/her life unto God. God is then very capable of speaking through these individuals. I know this to be a fact because it has worked in my life. Since I have been in the ministry I have gone before the judge on behalf of many people. God proved himself in the very moment that I spoke. I am not telling you not to retain counsel/lawyer. However, I have been able to convince the judge through my speech because God interceded. I got the victory. It works, but you must surrender your vessel unto God.

Chapter 48

HE IS THE COMFORTER

Let us go to **St John 14th** chapter. This is a promise of the spirit by Jesus Christ. He was speaking to his disciples in the Passover Chamber. We must remember at this time the disciples were very heavy hearted. We do not like to see our love ones leave home, nevertheless, these disciples had been with Christ and he is giving them the sad news that he is going to leave them. Jesus said:

St. John 14:16
And I will pray the father, and he shall give you another comforter, that he may abide with you forever;

Jesus used the term, "another comforter" because Jesus was a comforter. He walked, talked ate and fed his disciples. Remember the four thousand and the five thousand that he also fed?

St. Luke 9:16.
Then he took the five loaves and the two fishes, and looking up to heaven, he blessed them and brake, and gave to the disciples to set before the multitude.

Remember when they had to pay taxes? Jesus told Peter to go fishing.

St. Matthew 17:27.
Notwithstanding, lest we should offend them, go thou to the

sea, and cast an hook, and take up the fish that first cometh up; and when thou hast opened his mouth, thou shalt find a piece of money: that take, and give unto them for me and thee.

Jesus was always there whenever his disciples needed him. He was walking on the water when his disciples were in the ship afraid. Jesus said, be not afraid...

St. Matthew 14:25-31

And in the fourth watch of the night Jesus went unto them, walking on the sea. And when the disciples saw him walking on the sea, they were troubled, saying, It is a spirit; and they cried out for fear. But straightway Jesus spake unto them, saying, Be of good cheer; it is I; be not afraid. And Peter answered him and said, Lord, if it be thou, bid me come unto thee on the water. And he said, Come, And when Peter was come down out of the ship, he walked on the water, to go to Jesus. But when he saw the wind boisterous, he was afraid; and beginning to sink, he cried, saying, Lord, save me. And immediately Jesus stretched forth his hand, and caught him, and said unto him, O thou of little faith, wherefore didst thou doubt?

When Peter cried out Master, save me, Jesus did just that. The disciples learned to loved, to trust Jesus and to travel with Him in the ministry. They saw the miracles. Now Jesus begins telling them that He is going away and that He is going to give them another comforter. I always think of the Comforter as a heavy blanket in the cold winter time. When we get under that blanket we feel very comfortable and well satisfied. We do not care how the wind blows outside, we are content. It is such a time like this that the blanket has become our comforter. The Comforter is one of the names and attributes of the Holy Spirit. He is the comforter because he will comfort us if we allow Him to.

St. John 14:17-19:

Even the Spirit of truth; whom the world cannot receive, because it seeth him not, neither knoweth him: but ye know him; for he dwelleth with you, and shall be in you. I will not leave you comfortless: I will come to you. Yet a little while, and the world seeth me no more; but ye see me: because I live, ye shall live also.

Christ is saying that the world cannot receive the Comforter, because the world at large does not believe; neither do they honor God. The world's god is Satan. The Bible calls Satan the god of this world and the prince and the power of the air. All who are under the control of Satan cannot receive. They must come from under his control or have a desire to come from his control. Only then can an individual receive and see the Comforter. This is why the gospel is preached that we might tell mankind that there is a better way. He does not have to be bound by Satan.

St. John 14:26:

But the Comforter, which is the Holy Ghost, whom the Father will send in my name, he shall teach you all things, and bring all things to your remembrance, whatsoever I have said unto you.

Notice that he said , "whatsoever I said unto you..." We find people saying, as soon as they receive the Holy Ghost, that no one can tell them anything anymore. They have everything they need, but no so. Jesus said, as he spoke unto his disciples, *"the Holy Spirit will bring all things to your remembrance."* This is why Apostle Paul told Timothy:

2 Timothy 2:15.

Study to show thyself approved unto God, a workman that needeth not to be ashamed, rightly dividing the word of truth.

We must study! When we study, as the Lord said to Ezekiel, *"Eat the whole roll,"* we get God's word in us. Then the Holy Spirit will bring back to our remembrance that which God has placed in our hearts. David said:

Psalms 119:11.

Thy word have I hid in mine heart, that I might not sin against thee.

Therefore, just when we need the word of God, the Comforter will bring it to our remembrance. It is important to remember this, we do not stand on our own. We stand on the Comforter.

St. John 15:26:

But when the Comforter is come, whom I will send unto your from the Father, even the Spirit of truth, which proceedeth from the Father, he shall testify of me; And ye also shall bear witness because ye have been with me from the beginning.

The Comforter testifies of Jesus Christ.

I Corinthians 12:3:

Wherefore, I give you to understand, that no man speaking by the Spirit of God calleth Jesus accursed: and that no man can say that Jesus is the Lord but by the Holy Ghost.

Therefore if you hear a spirit anywhere speaking evil against Jesus, it is not the Holy Ghost. Just be aware and watch because it is of the Devil. The Holy Ghost will never speak contrary about Jesus Christ. The word of God bears witness to this.

Will you ask you to recognize that no man is able . . . and sometimes acquired such no . . . . . . one . . . . . . and the battle . . . . O . . .

. . . . . . to . . . a simple woman, sin and . . . . it is not the Holy Ghost that has me and . . . . . . in . . . it is in the Holy Ghost will leave . . . . Jesus . . . the word of God and . . . . . . to this . . .

Chapter 49

HE IS THE REPROVER

St. John 16:7-11:

Nevertheless I tell you the truth; it is expedient for you that I go away: for if I go not away, the Comforter will not come unto you; but if I depart, I will send him unto you. And when he is come, he will reprove the world of sin, and of righteousness, and of judgment: Of sin, because they believe not on me; Of righteousness, because I go to my father, and ye see me no more; Of judgment, because the prince of this world is judged.

This is the work of the Holy Spirit. Why would Jesus say that it was expedient for Him to go away? If He remained here on earth, the Comforter would not come. This is the Holy Ghost dispensation, and He is in control. Wherever we find sin the Holy Ghost will move against it. I can speak from experience. I had arthritis in my body fourteen miserable years. Because of sin, arthritis had taken over my body. This is the way that God was reproving me of my sins. When I made up my mind that I would give God my life, then He came in and healed my body and filled me with the Holy Spirit. I believe if I had not had arthritis I still would continue to go on my merry way. Many of you reading this manual can identify with what I am writing. You know what happened to you, and you know what it took to bring you to Christ. Maybe some of you reading have not received the Holy Spirit and may be you are having these problems. If you turn and ask God to put his Spirit in you, he will surely do it. Just ask! Let us look at what Luke, the physician, had to say concerning those that ask for the Holy Spirit:

St Luke 11:11-13.

If a son shall ask bread of any of you that is a father, will he give him a stone? or if he ask a fish, will he for a fish give him a serpent? or if he shall ask an egg, will he offer him a scorpion? If ye then, being evil, know how to give good gifts unto your children: how much more shall your heavenly Father give the Holy Spirit to them that ask him?

Yes! The Holy Ghost is the reprover of sin and of righteousness. Day by day God wants us to grow and become more righteous. What we did negative yesterday, God does not want us to do today. We must be as the Apostle Paul said.

I Corinthians 15:31.

In Christ Jesus Our Lord, I die daily

What is Apostle Paul actually saying to us? In other words, he is telling us to put off this daily walk and our fleshly ways. Day by day we are getting closer and closer to God because God is perfecting us. Once the Holy Spirit comes into us He begins to reprove us and make us more righteous. I like to think about what happens when we are buying a home or moving into an apartment and we begin to paint the walls, throw out things in the house that we don't like we change the furniture. What are we doing? We are reproving that house or apartment. This is the same thing the Holy Spirit does when he comes in. He makes us what God wants us to be.

260

St. John 16:8-11

When he [the Holy Spirit] *is come, he will reprove the world of sin, and of righteousness, and of judgment: Of sin, because they believe not on me; Of righteousness because I go to my Father, and ye see me no more.* [He goes to the Father and He works in us]. *Of judgment because the prince* [the Devil] *of this world is judged.*

Jesus said in the 12th verse:

I have yet many things to say unto you, but ye cannot bear them now. Howbeit when he, the Spirit of truth is come, he will guide you into all truth: for he shall not speak of himself; but whatsoever he shall hear, that shall he speak: and he will shew you things to come. He shall glorify me: for he shall receive of mine, and shall shew it unto you.

He is saying that the Spirit of Truth, which is the Holy Ghost will guide you into all truth. How many times has God made you to know something, and all of a sudden He illuminated your mind. You were enlightened and given this knowledge all of a sudden. Was there ever something you started to do and He told you not to do it. This is how the Spirit of God works in us. He will take the things of Christ, the words, the actions of Christ and reveal them unto us. This is the purpose of the Holy Spirit. I want you to understand this, because sometimes we just run away with this thing and say the Holy Ghost just gives us power. The Holy spirit is more than just giving us power. He is working in our lives, our thoughts and in our bodies. If we let the Holy Spirit have complete control, He works in all portions of our lives. Sometimes we say, "I surrender" and the Holy Spirit does not have complete control. To be totally surrendered He must have complete control of every part of

261

our body. We thank God for the Comforter.

Chapter 50

HE IS A SEARCHER

I Corinthians 2:9-12:

But as it is written, Eye hath not seen, nor ear heard, neither have it entered into the heart of man, the things which God hath prepared for them that love him. But God hath revealed them unto us by his Spirit: for the Spirit searcheth all things, yea, the deep things of God. For what man knoweth the things of a man, save the spirit of man which is in him? even so the things of God knoweth no man, but the Spirit of God. Now we have received, not the spirit of the world, but the spirit which is of God; that we might know the things that are freely given to us of God.

The word of God has just shown us that the Spirit is a searcher. Remember Jesus said:

St. John 16:13

Howbeit when he, the Spirit of truth is come, he will guide you into all truth: for he shall not speak of himself: but whatsoever he shall hear, that shall he speak: and he will shew you things to come.

The Holy Spirit searches reveals and he comforts. He is able to reveal certain things unto us. Sometimes you may hear someone say that God revealed this unto me. It is God through the Holy Ghost that does the revealing. It is just as it is recorded in the book of **Acts.**

Acts 1:2:

...after that He (Jesus) through the Holy Ghost had given commandments unto the apostles whom he had chosen.

Through the Holy Ghost, God will reveal many things to us. God is able to work through man by the Holy Ghost. The book of Acts is the Holy Ghost in action, guiding, calling, anointing, preparing men and revealing things to men that were to take place in the lives of men.

- Guides
- Calls
- Anoints
- Searches
- Reveals
- Comforter
- Reprover
- Prepare

THE HOLY GHOST

Chapter 51

THE HOLY SPIRIT IS A REVEALER

I Corinthians 2:10-11
But God hath revealed them unto us by his Spirit: for the Spirit searcheth all things, yea, the deep things of God. For what man knoweth the things of a man, save the spirit of man which is in him? even so the things of God knoweth no man, but the Spirit of God.

The spirit of man is the will and desire of man. Everyone of us has a spirit. You may have heard this saying by those who have animals, "I will break the spirit of this horse or mule so that I might be able to work him." In other words the will of the animal must be broken. When that will is broken, the will of the master, or (whoever is going to work or ride the animal) takes over.

There is a spirit of man and there is the Spirit of God. Let's look at a portion of **1 Corinthians 2:11** again:

Even so the things of God knoweth no man, but the Spirit of God.

We do not know the will of God but if the Holy Ghost reveals him unto us then we know the will of God. We rely upon the Holy Ghost, as the Scriptures says, to lead and guide us into all truths:

St. John 16:13.
...when the Spirit of truth is come, he will guide you in all truth.

265

Therefore, some of the functions of the Holy Ghost are to **comfort**, to **reveal**, to **lead**, to **guide**, to **teach** and to **search** the deep things of God. He plays a major part in our salvation. It is very important that each child of God knows what he has when he receives the Holy Spirit.

I Corinthians 2:12
Now we have received, not the spirit of the world, but the spirit which is of God; that we might know the things that are freely given to us of God.

St. John 4:24.
God is Spirit and they that worship him must worship him in spirit and in truth.

Let us continue in **I Corinthians 2:14:**
But the natural man receiveth not the things of the Spirit of God: for they are foolishness unto him: neither can he know them, because they are spiritually discerned.

Let us go to to where we again find the Holy Ghost as a revealer.

St. Mark 12:35-37.
And Jesus answered and said, while he taught in the temple, How say the scribes that Christ is the Son of David? For David himself said by the Holy Ghost, The Lord said to my Lord, Sit thou on my right hand, till I make thine enemies thy footstool. David therefore himself calleth him Lord; and whence is he then his son? And the common people heard him gladly.

David in the Spirit, (Holy Ghost within him) had seen Jesus and called him Lord. The people are calling him the son of David. Rightfully so, because Jesus Christ called himself the son of David and the son of man, meaning the son of David. The word says:

St. Matthew 1:21
...and thou shalt call his name Jesus: and he shall save his people from their sins.

The name Jesus is his earthly name. Again, I repeat, David is saying by the Spirit,

St. Mark 12:36
The Lord said to my Lord, Sit thou on my right hand, till I make thine enemies thy footstool.

The word of God backs up this portion of Scripture that my Lord, whom David is speaking about it Jesus Christ and His Lord is God; Again, I will be repetitious in saying that God is saying to Jesus,

Sit thou on my right hand, till I make thine enemies thy footstool.

Let us look at another portion of Scripture verifying that Jesus ascended into heaven, and is sitting on the right hand of God:

St. Mark 16:19.
So then after the Lord had spoken unto them, he was received up into heaven, and sat on the right hand of God.

Also, Stephen, being full of the Holy Ghost, when he was stoned, looked up to heaven and saw Jesus on the right hand of God.

Acts 7:55-56

But, he, (Stephen) being full of the Holy ghost looked up stedfastly into heaven, and saw the glory of God, and Jesus standing on the right hand of God. And said, Behold, I see the heavens opened, and the Son of man standing on the right hand of God.

You will find people arguing or trying to discredit the fact that Jesus sat on the right hand of God. However, this is what the Bible teaches. There we will see the Father, Son and the Holy Ghost. Some believe it is Jesus Only. Yes we do know that Jesus is Diety. But there is one God in three divine personalities.

For example; Man (humanity) has a body, mind, and a soul, which we call spirit. God breathed into the physical body of Adam and Adam became a living soul (meaning life) Our breath is our life. When we receive the Holy Spirit, God fuses the Holy Spirit with our spirit and we become one in Christ and he can direct our lives. Remember the word of God says:

Romans 8:14

For as many as are led by the Spirit of God, they are the sons of God.

HE SPEAKS TRUTH
St. John 16:13-14

Howbeit when he, the Spirit of truth, is come, he will guide you into all truth: for he shall not speak of himself, but whatsoever he shall hear, that shall he speak: and he will shew you things to come. He shall glorify me: (Jesus) for he shall receive of mine, and shall shew it unto you.

268

Chapter 52

JESUS BREATHED ON THEM

St. John 20:22:
And when he had said this, he breathed on them, and saith unto them, Receive ye the Holy Ghost: Whose soever sins ye remit, they are remitted unto them; and whose soever sins ye retain, they are retained.

This is what people wonder about. What happened to the disciples when Jesus breathed on them and said:

Receive ye the Holy Ghost.

Did they receive the Holy Ghost? I always like to think of this as ground work. One puts the seed in the ground and he knows that the seed is coming up. He knows because the seed is there. When Jesus breathed on his disciples and said, *"Receive ye the Holy Ghost,"* that was the ground work. It was the day of Pentecost that brought in the fulfillment of the ground work Jesus did. Sometimes people say that they do not have to speak in tongues when they receive the Holy Ghost because the disciples did not speak in tongues when Jesus said, *"Receive ye the Holy Ghost."* They could not have received the Holy Ghost because the Comforter had not come.

The word of God says that tongues are for a sign.

I Corinthians 14:22
Wherefore tongues are for a sign, not to them that believe,

but to them that believe not;

WAITING FOR THE PROMISE

Although the disciples did not receive the Holy Ghost at this time, it was a preparation. They were waiting for the promise. Remember what Jesus told his disciples:

St. John 16:7

Nevertheless I tell you the truth; it is expedient for you that I go away: if I go not away, the Comforter will not come unto you; but if I depart, I will send him unto you.

You see at this time the Comforter had not come, but as I have already stated this was a preparation for the coming of the Holy Ghost. This was the ground work.

Let us go to the 1st chapter of Acts. There is a portion of Scriptures that I love to speak and to write about. It is after the resurrection of Jesus Christ.

Acts 1:1-5

The former treatise, have I made, O Theophilus, of all that Jesus began both to do and teach, Until the day in which he was taken up, after that he through the Holy Ghost had given commandments unto the apostles whom he had chosen: To whom also he shewed himself alive after his passion by many infallible proofs, being seen of them forty days, and speaking of the things pertaining to the kingdom of God: And being assembled together with them, commanded them that they should not depart from Jerusalem, but wait for the promise of the Father, which, saith he, ye have heard of me. For John truly baptized with water; but ye shall be baptized with the Holy Ghost not many days hence.

Jesus was quoting John the Baptist because John truly baptized with water. We have two baptism here, the water baptism, which is the works of John and the Holy Ghost Baptism which, as John said, is Jesus' baptism.

YE SHALL RECEIVE POWER

Before we go any further in this study, I would like to move ahead to **Acts 1:8**:

But ye shall receive power, after that the Holy Ghost is come upon you: and ye shall be witnesses unto me both in Jerusalem, and in all Judea, and in Samaria, and unto the uttermost part of the earth.

Now Jesus is saying to his disciples that ye shall receive the power of God, after the Holy Ghost is come upon you. And when you have this power, you will be my witnesses unto the uttermost parts of the earth, starting in Jerusalem. We cannot be a witness for Jesus unless we have the Holy Ghost. Apostle Peter wrote this to the church.

I Peter 4:11

If any man speak, let him speak as the oracles of God; if any man minister, let him do it as of the ability which God giveth: that God in all things may be glorified through Christ Jesus, to whom be praise and dominion for ever and ever. Amen

THOSE THAT ASK

The gospel according to St. Luke will complete our study on "The Works Of The Holy Spirit":

St. Luke 11:11

If a son shall ask bread of any of you that is a father, will he give him a stone? Or if he ask a fish, will he for a fish give him a serpent? Or if he shall ask an egg, will he offer him a scorpion? If ye then, being evil,. Know how to give good gifts unto your children: how much more shall your heavenly father give the Holy Spirit to them that ask him?

Understand what Jesus is saying. If our children come and ask us for bread, we definitely would not give them a stone. If they asked for a fish, would we turn around and give them a snake? No, definitely not! If they ask for an egg, would we give them a scorpion? No! Then as Jesus said, if ye then being evil (meaning not righteous) know how to give good gifts unto your children, how much more shall your Heavenly Father give the Holy Spirit to them who ask him. Therefore, all you have to do is make up your mind and ask God for the Holy Spirit and He will do the rest. God will open up a way. We don't always know how, but, he is able to send you to a place where you can receive the Holy Spirit. Maybe you do not know a full gospel church where the word is exercised in its fullness, however, God will open a door some way and you will have a chance to receive the baptism of the Holy Spirit.

PART XIII

THOSE THAT RESIST

THE HOLY GHOST

Chapter 53

RESISTING THE HOLY GHOST

God's word is so wonderful that we can go from one Scripture to another to prove his word. Right now we are going over to Acts 7th chapter where we will find those resisting the Holy Ghost. All over the world today, we can find people still resisting the Holy Ghost just as it was in Biblical times. Some are saying it does not take all of that, while others are saying I don't need the Holy Ghost. Then you have some that will tell you that they spoke to their pastor and he said, that is not for our religion, that is for the Pentecostal people. All of this is resisting the Holy Ghost. However, let us read what the word of God is saying:

Acts 7:51-53:

Ye stiffnecked and uncircumcised in heart and ears, ye do always resist the Holy Ghost: as your father did, so do ye. Which of the prophets have not your father persecuted? And they have slain them which shewed before of the coming of the Just One;(Jesus) of whom ye have been now the betrayers and murderers: Who have received the law by the disposition of angels, and have not kept it..

Therefore, they resisted the Holy Ghost continually.

THE STONING OF STEPHEN
Acts 7:54-59

When they heard these things they were cut to the heart, and they gnashed on him with their teeth. But he, [Steven]

275

being full of the Holy Ghost, looked stedfastly into heaven, and saw the glory of God, and Jesus standing on the right hand of God. And said, Behold, I see the heavens opened, and the Son of man standing on the right hand of God. Then they cried out with a loud voice, and stopped their ears, and ran upon him with one accord, And cast him out of the city, and stoned him: and the witness laid down their clothes at a young man's feet whose name was Saul. [This was Saul of Tarsus, aka Paul.] *And they stoned Stephen, calling upon God, and saying, Lord Jesus, receive my spirit.*

LORD JESUS RECEIVE MY SPIRIT

The only way, Stephen could say receive my Spirit is because he had received the baptism of the Holy Spirit and he belonged to God. As Apostle Paul said:

Ephesians 4:30
whereby, ye are sealed unto the day of redemption.

Let us continue with
Acts 7:60
And he kneeled down, and cried with a loud voice, Lord, lay not this sin to their charge. And when had said this, he fell asleep.

When we are in Christ, we do not die, the flesh goes back to the earth, but our spirit lives continuously. We fall asleep.

Chapter 54

THE DAY OF PENTECOST

It is very important that we go to the 2nd chapter of Acts 1st verse. Many times people will apply this chapter to Pentecostals only. But I again repeat, I am reading this as it is written and it is for all of us today.

Acts 2:1-6

And when the day of Pentecost was fully come, they were all with one accord in one place. And suddenly there came a sound from heaven as of a rushing mighty wind, and it filled all the house where they were sitting. And there appeared unto them cloven tongues as of fire, and it sat upon each of them. And they were all filled with the Holy Ghost, and began to speak with other tongues, as the Spirit gave them utterance. And there dwelling at Jerusalem Jews, devout men, out of every nation under heaven. Now when this was noised abroad, the multitude came together, and were confounded, because that every man heard them speak in his own language.

We must understand this. These were men from every nation under heaven. And every man heard them speak in their language. The Bible does not say it was the language of the apostles. Many people do not believe in speaking in tongues. However, God has granted this power to these Galileans to speak in tongues (languages) of other nations. Many have tried to discredit this portion of Scripture. But if you notice the 7th verse:

Acts 2:7-13

And they were all amazed and marvelled, saying one to another, Behold are not all these which speak Galileans? And how hear we every man in our own tongue, wherein we were born? Parthians, and Medes, and Elamites, and the dwellers in Mesopotamia, and in Judea, and Cappadocia, in Pontus, and Asia, Phrygia, and Pamphylia, in Egypt, and in the parts of Libya about Cyrene, and strangers of Rome, Jews and proselytes, Cretes and Arabians, we do hear them speak in our own tongues the wonderful works of God. And they were all amazed and were in doubt, saying one to another, What meaneth this? Others mocking said, These men are full of new wine.

No doubt you have heard people mock saints because of their salvation. We are called holy rollers and other such names. Maybe you have mocked others yourself in days gone by. Perhaps you have said "they must be crazy," they are speaking in tongues. Some try to discredit it and call it jibberish, however, this is the wonderful works of God. Remember others also mocked the disciples saying that they were full of new wine:

Acts 2:13-18

Others mocking said, These men are full of new wine. But Peter, standing up with the eleven, lifted up his voice, and said unto them, Ye men of Judea, and all ye that dwell at Jerusalem, be this known unto you, and hearken to my words. For these are not drunken as ye suppose, seeing it is but the third hour of the. But this is that which was spoken by the prophet Joel: And it shall come to pass in the last days, saith God, I will pour out of my Spirit upon

278

all flesh: and your sons and your daughters shall prophesy, and your young men shall see visions, and your old men shall dream dreams: And on my servants and on my handmaidens I will pour out in those days of my Spirit; and they shall prophesy.

Understand this: Many times people will say that everybody has the Holy Ghost, because God has poured out his Spirit upon all flesh. Remember, in the beginning of this study, I spoke and wrote about how God's Spirit strove with men of old. The Spirit of God came upon Saul and he prophesied:

1 Samuel 10:10-11
And when they came thither to the hill, .behold, a company of prophets met him; and the Spirit of God came upon him, and he [Saul] prophesied among them. And it came to pass, when all that knew him beforetime saw that, behold, he prophesied among the prophets, then the people said one to another, What is this that is come unto the son Kish? Is Saul also among the prophets?

David said in **Psalms 51:10**
...create in me a clean heart, O God; and renew a right spirit within me.

The right spirit was the spirit of Holiness, which is the Holy Spirit. The Spirit of God came upon the men of old. A few of them had the Holy Ghost. Today, God says I am going to pour out my spirit upon all flesh regardless of who you are. You can be a servant, handmaid, etc. God is now pouring out His spirit without respect of persons. In other words God is saying I am going to fill you with my Spirit.

279

Man cannot say I am a preacher and I have the Holy Ghost, but the Holy Ghost is not for you in the seats. Yes, it is for the ones in the seats.

Acts 2:39

For the promise is unto you, and to your children, and to all that are a far off, even as many as the Lord God shall call.

THOSE IN THE UPPER ROOM

Let us look at **Acts 1:12-14:**

Then returned they unto Jerusalem from the mount called Olivet which is from Jerusalem a sabbath's day's journey. And when they were come in they went up into an upper room where abode both Peter, and James and John and Andrew, Philip and Thomas. Bartholomew, and Matthew, James the son Alphaeus and Simon Zelotes, and Judas the brother of James. These all continued with one accord in prayer and supplication with the women and Mary the mother of Jesus, and with his brethren.

They all were there in the upper room and Mary the mother of Jesus; The one who brought Jesus Christ into the world in the flesh. She too was in the upper room along with her other children, Jesus brethren. Yes, Mary had other children. I am placing the following Scriptures to prove that this is so.

St. Matthew 13:55-57:

Is not this the carpenter's son? [Jesus Christ, Son of Joseph] *is not his mother called Mary? And his brethren, James, and Joses, and Simon and Judas? And his sisters, are they not all with us? Whence then hath this man all these things? And they were all offended in him, But Jesus said unto them, A prophet is not without honour, save in his own country, and in his own house.*

JOEL'S PROPHECY FULFILLED

Let us continue with **Acts 2:17-18**:
And it shall come to pass in the last days, saith God, I will pour out of my Spirit upon all flesh: and your sons and your daughters shall prophesy.
[meaning to foretell things which shall come to pass.]
And your young men shall see visions,
[meaning when you are awake and you can see very clearly. A dream is when you are asleep.]
And the old men shall dream dreams: And on my servants and on my handmaidens I will pour out in those days of my Spirit, and they shall prophesy
Prophesy also is rendered preaching, therefore God moved by his Spirit.

Chapter 55

THE EFFECT OF THE HOLY SPIRIT UPON APOSTLE PAUL

Let us look at the effect the Holy Spirit had upon Saul, also known as Apostle Paul.

Acts 9:26-31

And when *Saul was come to Jerusalem, he assayed to join himself to the disciples; but they were all afraid of him, and believed not that he was a disciple. But Barnabas took him, and brought him to the apostles, and declared unto them how he had seen the Lord in the way, and that he had spoken to him, and how he had preached boldly at Damascus in the name of Jesus. And he was with them coming in and going out Jerusalem. And he spake boldly in the name of the Lord Jesus, and disputed against the Grecians: but they went about to slay him. Which when the brethren knew, they brought him down to Caesarea, and sent him forth to Tarsus. Then had the churches rest throughout all Judea and Galilee and Samaria, and were edified; and walking in the fear of the Lord, and in the comfort of the Holy Ghost, were multiplied.*

This is after the conversion of Saul of Tarsus. The word Saul is the Hebrew name for Paul. Paul is Greek. It is English, but a Greek term. Saul and Paul are the same names. The church walked in peace after the conversion of Saul. Before his conversion Saul persecuted the church on every hand. If you notice, the word says that they walked in the comfort of the Holy Ghost. Remember Jesus called the Holy Ghost the Comforter and the Spirit of Truth. Now we see the church walking in the comfort of the Holy Ghost. All of us love to walk in the comfort of the Holy Ghost. Jesus also said:

St John 14:27
My Peace I leave with you, my peace I give unto you: not as the world giveth, give I unto you. Let not your heart be troubled, neither let it be afraid.

Therefore, the word proves that we can walk in this comfort and peace. This is to all those who are in Christ Jesus. We have made up our minds. This is why Apostle Paul said:

Philippians 4:11
Not that I speak in respect of want: for I have learned, in whatsoever state I am , therewith to be content.

We learn to be content by the power of the Holy Ghost. If the fruit of the Spirit is working in our lives we then become peaceful saints in Christ. When we have reached this, we have crucified the flesh.

Chapter 56

THE FRUIT OF THE SPIRIT

Let us go on to **Galatians 5:22-23**
But the fruit of the Spirit is
"love,"
(this is the manifestation and the works of the Spirit of God.
Jesus said:

St. John 13:35
By this shall all men know that ye are my disciples, if ye have love one to another.

We must also study the greatest chapter written on love which is the Thirteenth Chapter of **1st Corinthians**. The church at Corinth was coveting the gifts. However, Apostle Paul told them these words:

I Corinthians 12:31
But covet earnestly the best gift: and yet I show unto you a more excellent way.

The more excellent way is love. It is important that we have love for one another. We do not love by the flesh, but we love by the Spirit of God.

"joy,"
The Holy Ghost gives us joy which does not depend upon circumstances. Let us see what the word says about joy.

Nehemiah 8:10
The joy of the Lord is your strength.

"peace,"

Jesus told his disciples:

St. John 14:27

Peace I leave with you, my peace I give unto you, not as the world giveth, give I unto you. Let not your heart be troubled neither let it be afraid.

"longsuffering,"

Longsuffering means to suffer long and to wait.

Job 14:14:

...all the days of my appointed time will I wait until my change come.

In other words Job is saying, if it take all of my life I am going to wait, today, tomorrow, I will wait. God is a longsuffering God. He tolerates us in our sins for so many years. God waits for us to get a change of mind. Even after we come to him, we still go contrary to his word. Nevertheless God is still patient with us and continues to draw us if we desire to do that which is good.

"gentleness,"

Gentleness is the opposite of boasting. Many times we refer to a saint as a sheep and/or a lamb. However, we must look at the goat. He is a pretty rough creature. He will ram you and he will eat most anything. He is a contrary animal. But the lamb is very meek and easy to be intreated. He is a very gentle creature.

"goodness,"

Goodness is kindness, being agreeable, pleasant, easy to be intreated and virtuous. The word of God says:

Galatians 6:10
*As we have opportunity, let us do **good** unto all men, especially unto them who are of the household of faith*

Psalms 37:23
*The steps of a **good** man are ordered by the Lord: and he delighteth in his way.*

Proverbs 12:2
*A **good** man obtaineth favour of the Lord; but a man of wicked devices will be condemned.*

"faith,"
Romans 12:3.
God hath dealt to every man the measure of faith:

Hebrews 11:6.
Without faith it is impossible to please God.

Therefore, we must manifest the fruit of faith. Faith is also a gift of the Spirit. (Read **I Corinthians 12:1-11**). James stated:

James 2:17-20
Even so faith, if it hath not works, is dead, being alone. Yea, a man may say, Thou hast faith, and I have works: shew me thy faith, without thy works, and I will shew thee my faith by my works. Thou believest that there is one God; thou doest well: the devils also believe and tremble. But wilt thou know, O vain man, that faith without works is dead.

"meekness,"
The Bible speaks about the meekness, (meaning humility) of Moses.

Numbers 12:3.

Now the man Moses was very meek, above all the men which were upon the face of the earth.

This is a pretty good report. We look at the trials and the tribulations of Moses, who remained a meek and humble man. The last fruit of the Spirit is:

"temperance,"

...against such there is no law. And they that are in Christ's have crucified the flesh with the affections and lusts. If we live in the Spirit, let us also walk in the Spirit. Let us not be desirous of vain glory, provoking one another, envying one another.

The word of God has just proven to us that there are fruits of the Spirit and there are fruits of the flesh. I repeat, when we have reached this, we have crucified the flesh.

Chapter 57

FORBIDDEN BY THE HOLY GHOST

Let us look at another function of the Holy Spirit.

Acts 16:6-8:
Now when they had gone throughout Phrygia and the region of Galatia, and were forbidden of the Holy Ghost to preach the word in Asia. After they were come to Mysia, they assayed to go into Bithynia: but the Spirit suffered them not. And they passing by Mysia came down to Troas.

Here again we see the function of the Holy Spirit. He forbid them to preach in Asia. I know this because I witnessed it myself. At some times in visiting the hospitals, the Holy Spirit would forbid me to stop in certain rooms or certain beds. I learned to bypass these rooms or a particular bed and 'go on to the next patient as the Lord would lead. Always be sure it is the Holy Spirit directing you. Sometimes we say the Holy Spirit did not lead me to do this. However, I am talking about when the Holy Spirit has a strong hand upon you, then will you know. If you ever want to make a bad mistake, overide the Holy Spirit when he tells you to pass by a person or do not deal with that individual. Although you heard the Holy Spirit, you go anyway. Sometimes you will experience the person cursing you out. "I don't want your prayers..." "I don't believe in your God." I have seen it happen so many times. When the Holy Spirit leads us and we do as the Holy Spirit tells us we cannot go wrong because the Holy Spirit knows the heart and the mind of every individual.

It may seem strange to you that God told His servants not to preach in Asia. God had another place for Apostle Paul to preach at that particular time, because God knew very well that they would not receive him in Asia.

Chapter 58

HAVE YOU RECEIVED THE HOLY GHOST SINCE YOU BELIEVED?

Acts 19:1 is an important portion of Scripture to me. I cannot preach it, teach it or write about it enough, because we find people from all walks of life that do not believe that the Holy Ghost is necessary. They are leaning toward their own righteousness, saying, "I've done what God told me to do. I was baptized," and they take the water baptism and go on about their business.

Acts 19:1-7

And it came to pass, that, while Apollos was at Corinth, Paul having passed through the upper coasts came to Ephesus: and finding certain disciples, He said unto them, Have ye received the Holy Ghost since ye believed? And they said unto him, we have not so much as heard whether there be any Holy Ghost. And he said unto them, Unto what then were ye baptized? And they said, Unto John's baptism. Then said Paul, John verily baptized with the baptism of repentance, saying unto the people, that they should believe on him which should come after him, that is, on Christ Jesus. When they heard this, they were baptized in the name of the Lord Jesus. And when Paul had laid his hands upon them, the Holy Ghost came on them; and they spake with tongues and prophesied. And all the men were about twelve.

These men were believers, but they had only heard of

John's baptism. This is the same thing that happened in my life. I was baptized in water when I was 14 years old. I wanted to do God's will so very much. However, I found myself drifting back doing the same things I had done before. But when the arthritis took over my body at the age of 19 to 33 years, I made up my mind to turn to the living God and serve him. Then I was healed and received the Holy Ghost. I was 33 years old when I heard about the baptism of the Holy Ghost. It was preached to me just as John said:

St. Matthew 3:11

I indeed baptize you with water unto repentance: but he that cometh after me is mightier than I, whose shoes I am not worthy to bear: he shall baptize you with the Holy Ghost and with fire.

So Apostle Paul laid his hands on these men. Notice that they spoke in tongues as the Spirit of God gave utterance, and all the men were about twelve. It is very important to remember it is the Holy Ghost that does the work.

Chapter 59

APOLLOS - FERVENT IN THE SPIRIT

Let us go back to **Acts 18:** and see the mighty working of the Holy Spirit in one man's life.

ACTS 18:23-28

And after he [Apostle Paul] *had spent some time there, he departed, and went over all the country of Galatia and Phrygia in order, strengthening all the disciples. And a certain Jew named Apollos, born at Alexandria, an eloquent man, and mighty in the scriptures, came to Ephesus. This man was instructed in way of the Lord; and being fervent in the Spirit, he spake and taught diligently the things of the Lord, knowing only the baptism of John. And he began to speak boldly in the synagogue: whom when Aquila and Priscilla had heard, they took him unto them, and expounded unto him the way of God more perfectly. And when he was disposed to pass into Achaia, the brethren wrote, exhorting the disciples to receive him: who, when he was come, helped them much which had believed through grace. For he mightly convinced the Jews and that publickly shewing by the scriptures that Jesus was Christ.*

Notice that the word says that this man was fervent in the spirit and he taught the things that be of God. But he knew only John's baptism, which is the water baptism. I have seen many preachers that could stand and preach you happy. These preachers would get joy after they get warmed up and they could make you feel good. The Spirit would come upon them and they would really preach. It does not mean that they have been filled with the Holy Ghost. There is a difference. I remember as a boy, I went to the mourners' bench, and I felt real good when they baptized me in the water. I remember one of my friends felt so good, he leaped up and went running out of the church to go home and tell "momma" that he had 'got religion.' Now, don't mix up religion with the Holy Ghost. Religion is when the Spirit comes upon you and you get happy. The Holy Ghost is in you. Regardless of how you feel, He is in you. God promised that he would not write His word word upon plaques of stone, but He would write them in the hearts of men God promised to walk in us and talk in us. He would be our God and we would be His sons and his daughters. Through the word of God, I want you to understand what the baptism of the Holy Ghost is all about. By now I pray that you have an understanding of the difference between the two baptisms; the water baptism and the baptism of the Holy Ghost. The conclusion of the whole matter is this, the water baptism was for the remission of sins. This is the 6th dispensation, "Grace" and God forgives us of our sins. We are not under the law.

Chapter 60

THE KINGDOM OF GOD IS...
RIGHTEOUSESS, JOY AND PEACE
IN THE HOLY GHOST

Let us go to **Romans 14.** This is another study all by itself. It is pertaining to meat and eating; what we should, or should not, eat. I mainly want to deal with the Holy Ghost, since this chapter is on the function of the Holy Spirit. However, I will bring out a few brief points.

ROMANS 14:17-18

But if thy brother be grieved with thy meat, now walkest thou not charitably, Destroy not him with thy meat, for whom Christ died. Let not then your good be evil spoken of. For the Kingdom of God is not meat and drink; but righteousness, and peace, and joy in the Holy Ghost.

Joy is one of the fruits of the spirit. We all would like to have joy. Joy is not when we are grinning constantly. Joy is an inner-satisfaction emotion deep down in our souls. We have peace in Jesus Christ our Lord. This gives us that inner security that we are right with our God. If we were to pass away at this time, we would be assured that heaven would be our home. This is joy! Sometimes this assurance comes to the outside and we find our soul is bubbling over and we can't help but praise and thank God for this inner joy and peace. Therefore, this is God's will for us,

For the Kingdom of God is not meat and drink; but righteousness, and peace, and joy in the Holy Ghost.

At this point, I find myself being repetitious, even reviewing some of the things I have previously written. Keep in mind, the purpose of these studies is for you to be able to follow them in your Bible. I have taking the time to put this study on tape, as well as in print, in xthat you will be able to follow along with me using your Bible. Remember we started out in the book of **Genesis.**

Genesis 1:2:
In the beginning God created the heaven and the earth and the earth was without form and void; and darkness was upon the face of the deep. And the Spirit of God moved upon the face of the waters.

We have already stated, that the Spirit of the Lord which moved upon the face of the waters was the Holy Spirit. He (the Holy Spirit) was functioning in the beginning with the works of the creation. The power of God controlled everything at that time. I have also written that the Holy Spirit was given to certain men at that time. In earlier Biblical times the Holy Spirit was not poured out upon all people.

As we go futher into this study, I will continue to make statements to prove the functioning and the necessity of the Holy Spirit. Sometimes we take the Holy Spirit very lightly. Some comment that the Holy Spirit gives us power, however, there are other functions of the Holy Spirit. Our aim is to let you know His purpose because he is the power of God.

Chapter 61

OIL IS SYMBOLIC OF
THE HOLY SPIRIT

Oil represents the Holy spirit, the power of God. This is why we have the parable of the ten virgins, five wise and five foolish. The wise virgins had oil in their lamps, meaning the Holy Spirit.

THE TEN VIRGINS
St. Matthew 25:1-13

Then shall the kingdom of heaven be likened unto ten virgins, which took their lamps and went forth to meet the bridegroom. And five of them were wise, and five were foolish. They that were foolish took their lamps and took no oil with them; But the wise took oil in their vessels with their lamps. While the bridegroom tarried they all slumbered and slept. And at midnight there was a cry made, Behold, the bridegroom cometh; go ye out to meet him. Then all those virgins arose, and trimmed their lamps. And the foolish said unto the wise, Give us of your oil; for our lamps are gone out. But the wise answered, saying, Not so; lest there be not enough for us and you: but go ye rather to them that sell, and buy for yourselves. And while they went to buy, the bridegroom came; and they that were ready went in with him to the marriage: and the door was shut. Afterward came also the other virgins, saying, Lord, Lord, open to us. But he answered and said, Verily, I say unto you, I know you not. Watch therefore, ye for you know neither the day nor the hour wherein the Son of man cometh.

Chapter 62

IF YOU HAVE NOT THE SPIRIT

The 12th verse states: "but he answered and said, Verily, I say unto you, I know you not." This verifies what the Apostle Paul stated in **Romans 8:9.** " *Now if any man have not the Spirit of Christ, he is none of his.* " This is why Jesus told Nicodemus…

St. John 3:3

Except a man be born again, he cannot see the kingdom of God.

I want you to understand the importance of the Holy Ghost, and the part He plays in our salvation. We hear so many arguments surrounding the new birth. So many people believe that when they receive the water baptism, that they have been born again. Some believe when they repeat the sinner's prayer, that they have been born again. However, let us clarify this with the word of God.

St. John 3:1-6

There was a man of the Pharisees, name Nicodemus, a ruler of the Jews: The same came to Jesus by night, and said unto him, Rabbi, we know that thou art a teacher come from God: for no man can do these miracles that thou doest, except God be with him. Jesus answered and said unto him, Verily, verily, I say unto thee, Except a man be born again, he cannot see the kingdom of God. Nicodemus saith unto him, How can a man be born when he is old?

can he enter the second time into his mother's womb, and be born. Jesus answered, Verily, verily, I say unto thee, Except a man be born of the water and of the Spirit, he cannot enter into the kingdom of God. That which is born of the flesh is flesh; and that which is born of the Spirit is spirit. Marvel not that I said unto thee, Ye must be born again.

This is very important to you because, as I stated before, many people believe they are saved and are on their way to heaven. These are the words of Jesus Christ. Therefore, we must go past the water baptism and go on to the spiritual baptism, which is Jesus' baptism. At this time, I am going to go in a different direction, but will return to this portion of Scripture. I find it necessary to back up this Scripture, with Scripture. Let us go over to the Gospel according to St. Mark 1, remembering that Jesus told Nicodemus:

Except a man be born of water and of the Spirit, he cannot enter into the kingdom of God.

It is important that we believe the word of God.

St. Mark 1:1-8

The beginning of the gospel of Jesus Christ, the Son of God; As it is written in the prophets, Behold, I send my messenger before my face, which shall prepare thy way before thee. The voice of one crying in the wilderness, Prepare ye the way of the Lord, make his paths straight. John did baptize in the wilderness, and preach the baptism of repentance for the remission of sins. And there went out unto him all the land of Judea, and they of Jerusalem, and were all baptized of him in the river of Jordan, confessing their sins. And John was clothed with camel's hair, and with a girdle of a skin about his loins; and he did eat locusts and wild honey; And preached saying, There cometh one mightier than I after me, the latchet of whose shoes I am not worthy to stoop down and unloose. I indeed have baptized you with water: but he shall baptize you with the Holy Ghost.

Jesus will baptize you with the Holy Ghost. I cannot write it or speak it enough. We must keep these two baptisms separate. The water baptism and the Holy Ghost baptism. Many times people will refer to the Holy Ghost baptism as a "gift." Yes it is a gift, meaning the Holy Ghost is given freely to us by God. The price was paid by Jesus Christ on Calvary.

I Corinthians 6:20
For ye are brought with a price: therefore glorify God in your body, and in your spirit which are God's.

Yes, it is a gift and the only thing required of you is to believe. Notice in the Gospel according to:

St. Mark 1:9-11:
And it came to pass in those days, that Jesus came from Nazareth of Galilee, and was baptized of John in Jordan. And straightway coming up out of the water, he saw the heavens opened, and the Spirit like a dove descending upon him: And there came a voice from heaven, saying, Thou art my beloved Son, in whom I am well pleased.

Jesus was baptized with the Holy Ghost simultaneously when he received the ritual of the Holy Spirit.

Let us go back to the portion of Scripture on Nicodemus: The above Scripture is exactly what Jesus is saying unto Nicodemus in **St. John 3rd chapter**.

Except a man be born of the water and of the Spirit, he cannot enter into the kingdom of God. That which is born of the flesh is flesh; and that which is born of the Spirit is spirit.

Our first birth was that of our mother and our father; the desires of the flesh. The second birth is through the baptism of the Holy Spirit. Yet, people say they are born again, although they have not received the baptism of the Holy Spirit. Some believe that once you confess Christ or make your decision for Christ, or accept Him in your heart, you are born again. This is not so. Understand what Jesus is saying. *"That which is born of the flesh is flesh Marvel not..."* in other words, do not be surprised; *"...that I said unto thee, Ye must be born again."*

Jesus gives us a good illustration in the **8th** verse of **St. John 3rd** Chapter. Let us read:

St. John 3:8
The wind bloweth where it listeth and thou hearest the sound thereof, but canst not tell whence it cometh, and whither it goeth: so is every one that is born of the Spirit.

In other words, we hear and feel the wind, we know that the wind is blowing, but we do not know at what point the wind started or at what point it stopped. Jesus likened this to every one that is born of the Spirit. We receive the baptism of the Holy Spirit; we feel Him moving in us and we know He came to us as we believed. However, we received the

Holy Spirit, we know the Holy Spirit came into us. But we do not know the beginning or the ending of the Holy Ghost. Notice that when Nicodemus came unto Jesus. He told Him, *Rabbi, we know that thou art a teacher come from God: for no man can do these miracles that thou doest, except God be with him.*

Jesus was putting the emphasis on the greater part. He did not say, "Nicodemus, I am glad you believe in the miracles that I am doing." Instead, Jesus explained to Nicodemus the greater part which is the new birth.

Let us now go to **St. John 4th** chapter which speaks to us about the woman at the well. At this time Jesus is offering the woman at the well, the living water which is the spiritual water. Jesus had a need to go through Samaria, because He knew, very well, that the woman would be coming to draw water. This is quite a study here, therefore, I will place these Scriptures in order that you might get the complete thought:

St. John 4:1-2
When therefore the Lord knew how the Pharisees had heard that Jesus made and baptized more disciples than John. (Though Jesus himself baptized not, but his disciples.)

Jesus did not baptized with water, His disciples did baptize. There is no place in your Bible where you find that Jesus baptized anyone with water. His baptism is the baptism of the Holy Ghost. Therefore his disciples were the ones baptizing.

He left Judea, and departed again into Galilee. And he

must needs go through Samaria. Then cometh he to a city of Samaria, which is called Sychar, near to the parcel of ground that Jacob gave to his son Joseph. Now Jacob's well was there. Jesus therefore, being wearied with his journey, sat thus on the well: and it was about the sixth hour [Twelve is high noon. Count from 6 a.m., which is the first hour, the sixth hour is 12:00]

St. John 3:4-10
There cometh a woman of Samaria [heathen woman— non-Jewish] *to draw water: Jesus saith unto her, Give me to drink. (For his disciples were gone away unto the city to buy meat.) Then saith the woman of Samaria unto him, How is it that thou being a Jew, askest drink of me, which am a woman of Samaria? for the Jews have no dealings with the Samaritans. Jesus answered and said unto her, If thou knewest the gift of God, and who it is that saith to thee, Give me to drink; thou wouldest have asked of him, and he would have given thee living water.*

This living water, which Jesus is speaking about, is the Holy Spirit. It is two-fold. Just as we cannot not live without the natural water, we cannot live without the spiritual water, meaning eternal (living) life. Therefore, the Holy Spirit is likened unto water. It is stated that over ninety percent of our body is water. Just as our bodies are a large percentage of water, when the Holy Spirit comes in, we should be consumed, not just ninety percent, but, one hundred percent by the Holy Ghost.

St. John 4:11-14:
The woman saith unto him, Sir, thou hast nothing to draw with, and the well is deep: from whence then hast thou that

living water? Art thou greater than our father Jacob, which gave us the well, and drank thereof himself, and his children, and his cattle? Jesus answered and said unto her, Whosoever drinketh of this water shall thirst again: But whosoever drinketh of the water that I shall give him shall never thirst; but the water that I shall give him shall be in him a well of water springing up into everlasting life.

Notice that Jesus said the water that I shall give him shall be a well of water, meaning plenty of water. The water will continue to flow and spring up into everlasting life. This is the association of the natural water and the Holy Spirit of life eternal. Yet so many are saying the Holy Ghost gives you power but it has nothing to do with our spiritual life. This is not so. The Holy Spirit is our spiritual life. Let us look at the **15th** and **16th** verses:

The woman saith unto him, Sir, give me this water, that I thirst not, neither come hither to draw. Jesus said unto her, Go, call thy husband, and come hither.

Notice that Jesus said unto her, "go call your husband and come hither." In other words there was something between this woman and her receiving this water; although she could not receive the spiritual water at this time because Jesus had not gone back to his Father and the Holy Ghost had not yet come. This was a preparation. However, she received the word, but she did not receive the Holy Ghost because Jesus said:

St. John 16:7
Nevertheless, it is expedient for you that I go away: for if I go not away, the Comforter will not come unto you; but if I depart, I will send him unto you.

The Comforter did come on the day of Pentecost. Therefore, at this time, Jesus is preparing the woman for the receiving of the Holy Spirit.

St. John 4:17-19:
The woman answered and said, I have no husband. Jesus said unto her, Thou has well said, I have no husband: Jesus said unto her, Thou hast well said, I have no husband: For thou hast had five husbands; and he whom thou now hast is not thy husband: in that saidst thou truly. The woman saith unto him, Sir, I perceive that thou art a prophet. Our father worshipped in this mountain; and ye say, that in Jerusalem is the place where men ought to worship.

If you look throughout the Old Testament you will see men worshipped God in the mountains. Abraham and many of the men of Biblical times went up into the mountains to worship, pray and offer up sacrifices unto God. Even the pagan gods were worshipped in the mountains. In Jerusalem, which is called the city of the great king, the people looked forward to coming and worshipping God. It was the custom of the Jews to come and worship on the day of Pentecost year by year. The great temple that Solomon built was in Jerusalem. That was the place for worship, however, Jesus is showing this woman something else. It was not the place that was important. At the 21st verse of the 4th chapter of St. John, Jesus said to the woman:

Woman, believe me, the hour cometh, when ye shall neither in this mountain, nor yet at Jerusalem, worship the Father.

Remember what I have written, that Jesus at this time

is preparing her for the Holy Spirit. He said the hour cometh: He did not say it is right now. Therefore, he is looking at Pentecost and beyond. This takes us to the **22**nd and the **23**rd verses:

Ye worship ye know not what: we know what we worship: for salvation is of the Jews. But the hour cometh, and now is, when the true worshippers shall worship the Father in spirit and in truth: for the Father seeketh such to worship him.

"But the hour cometh and now is" means the hour is come into manifestation by faith, that you will worship God not in the mountains nor in Jerusalem, but in Spirit and in truth.

St. John 4:24
God is a Spirit: and they that worship him must worship him in spirit and in truth.

Therefore, if you have not received the Holy Spirit, how can you worship God. You must worship him in Spirit and truth only. Jesus said:

St. John 14:6.
I am the way, the truth, and the life: no man cometh unto the Father, but by me.

This is why Jesus said to Nicodemus:

St. John 3:7.
Marvel not that I said unto thee, Ye must be born again.

Let us look at **St. John 4:25**:

The woman saith unto him, I know that Messias cometh, which is called Christ: when he is come, he will tell us all things. Jesus saith unto her, I that speak unto thee am he.

Understand that it was important that Jesus go through Samaria because he was aware of the needs that he wanted to take care of at this time.

Let us go to **Hebrews 3:7-12**. Here again we find information about the Holy Ghost.

Wherefore, (as the Holy Ghost saith, To day if ye will hear his voice, Harden not your hearts, as in the provocation, in the day of temptation in the wilderness: When your fathers tempted me, proved me, and saw my works forty years. Wherefore, I was grieved with that generation, and said, They do always err in their heart; and they have not know my ways. So I sware in my wrath, They shall not enter into my rest) Take heed, brethren, lest there be in any of you an evil heart of unbelief, in departing from the living God.

The word is saying in the 7th **verse** that the Holy Ghost speaks and if you hear his voice, harden not your heart. The Holy Ghost is speaking unto the church. Many times we look at the preacher. If the preacher is anointed by God speaking the word by the Spirit of God, with the anointing then the Holy Ghost is speaking unto you and/or the church. From time to time people will laugh and mock and will not believe that all of this is necessary, however, they are laughing and mocking the Holy Ghost. Instead of mocking, it is time to repent because if we do not hear God's voice, surely, he will cut us off. Again I repeat, when you hear the voice of the Lord speaking by the Holy Ghost do not harden your heart.

Let us go over to **Hebrews** where we again see the Holy Ghost in action.

Hebrews 6:4-6:

For it is impossible for those who were once enlightened, and have tasted of the heavenly gift, and were made partakers of the Holy Ghost, And have tasted the good word of God, and the powers of world to come, If they shall fall away, to renew them again unto repentance; seeing they crucify to themselves the Son God afresh, and put him to an open shame.

The word of God is speaking to those that have tasted of the heavenly gift, meaning the Holy Ghost, and were made partakers of the Holy Ghost. In order to be a partaker of the Holy Ghost, we must have received the Holy Ghost. In other words, you must not just say Holy Ghost but have received the Holy Ghost as they did on the day of Pentecost. You have then been made a partaker. Let me use this example for clarity. If I offer you a piece of cake and say share this with me, be a partaker, that means you must eat it. But as long as it is in your hand, you are not a partaker of it because it still remains in your hand. However, once you eat of it, the same as I am doing, only then are you a partaker. The word of God says:

Psalms 34:8

O taste and see that the Lord is good: blessed is the man that trusteth in him.

We taste of God and know that He is good when we receive the baptism of the Holy Ghost.

Let us now move on to **II Peter.**

II Peter 1:21:
For the prophecy came not in old time by the will of man: but by the holy men of God spake as they were moved by the Holy Ghost.

We see right in our Bibles, how God moved through us that we might speak by the Holy Ghost. This is why we have our Bibles revealing to us the prophecy pertaining to the suffering of Jesus Christ, as recorded in the book of Isaiah.

Isaiah 53:5:
But he was wounded for our transgressions, he was bruised for our iniquities: the chastisement of our peace was upon him; and with his stripes we are healed.

This and other Scriptures are truth. They are a fulfillment of the prophecies which came not in the old time by the will of men but by men as they were moved by the Holy Ghost.

We are going to **Romans 8ᵗʰ** chapter. This chapter is written to the spirit filled church of God. They have received the baptism of the Holy Ghost, speaking in tongues as the Spirit of God gives utterance. Let us read:

Romans 8:1
There is therefore now no condemnation to them which are in Christ Jesus, who walk not after the flesh, but after the Spirit.. For the law of the Spirit of life in Christ Jesus hath made me free from the law of sin and death. For what the law could not do, in that it was weak through the flesh, God sending his own Son in the likeness of sinful flesh, and for sin, condemned sin in the flesh: That the righteousness of

the law might be fulfilled in us, who walk not after the flesh, but after the Spirit.

Again the word of God is speaking about the Holy Ghost. There is a walk after the Holy Spirit and a walk after the flesh. Remember, Jesus said unto Nicodemus:

St. John 3:6.
That which is born of the flesh is flesh; and that which is born of the Spirit is spirit.

Also let us recall the words of John the Baptist:

St. Matthew 3:11
I indeed baptize you with water unto repentance: but he that cometh after me is mightier than I, whose shoes I am not worthy to bear: he shall baptize you with the Holy Ghost and fire...

We should readily see the flesh and the Spirit. Apostle Paul said:

Romans 8:1
There is therefore now no condemnation to them which are in Christ Jesus, who walk not after the flesh, but after the Spirit.
In other words walk not as a natural man, but walk as a spiritual man. As it is recorded in:

Philippians 2:5.
Let this mind be in you, which was also in Christ Jesus.

What was the mind of Christ Jesus? His mind was to

do the will of Him that sent Him. Jesus said:

St. John 5:30
I can of mine own self do nothing: as I hear, I judge: and my judgment is just, because I seek not mine own will, but the will of the Father which hath sent me.

Therefore, this portion of Scripture in Romans 8th chapter is letting us know that we, through Christ Jesus, are not condemned. When we get down to the last day, God cannot say unto us, depart from me you workers of iniquity, I never knew you. He cannot say this if we have been born again and are walking after the Spirit. Remember the earlier portion of this study where Jesus told the woman at the well:

St. John 4:24
God is a Spirit: and they that worship him must worship him in spirit and in truth.

Let us continue in **Romans 8:5:**
For they that are after the flesh do mind the things of the flesh; but they that are after the Spirit the things of the Spirit.

In other words, the following Scripture bears witnesss:

St. Luke 16:13.
No servant can serve two masters: for either he will hate the one, and love the other; or else he will hold to the one, and despise the other. Ye cannot serve God and mammon [meaning man].

We may find ourselves tossed and driven. The word of

God speaks on this wise:

James 1:8.
A double minded man is unstable in all his ways.

As Peter says, it is better to obey God rather than man. No, we cannot serve God and mammon (man.) Let us continue with **Romans 8:6:**
For to be carnally minded is death, but to be spiritually minded is life and peace.

Humanity is looking for peace, but cannot obtain peace without finding peace with God. Jesus spoke these words:

St. John 14:27
Peace I leave with you, my peace I give unto you: not as the world giveth, give I unto you. Let not your heart be troubled, neither let it be afraid.

Concerning life, Jesus also said:

St. John 14:6.
I am the way, the truth, and the life; no man cometh unto the Father, but by me.

Again, let me reiterate the words of the Apostle Paul:

Romans 8:6
But to be spiritually minded is life and peace.

Let us go on to **Romans 8:7-9**:
Because the carnal mind is enmity against God: for it is not subject to the law of God, neither indeed can be. So then they that are in the flesh cannot please God. But ye are not

in the flesh, but in the Spirit, if so be that the Spirit of God dwell in you. Now if any man have not the Spirit of Christ, he is none of his.

I have underlined this latter phrase, because you find many people saying, I am a child of God, however, Jesus told the Pharisees:

St. John 8:44-45, 47
Ye are of your father the devil, and the lusts of your father ye will do. He was a murderer from the beginning, and abode not in the truth, because there is no truth in him. When he a lie, he speaketh of his own, for he is a liar, and the father of it. And because I tell you the truth ye believe me not. He that is of God heareth God's words: ye therefore hear them not, because ye are not of God.

Therefore, God's word is pretty clear when he says:

Romans 8:9
Now of any man have not the Spirit of Christ, he is none of his.

God's word is making it plain that if anyone wants to be a child of His, he must have the Holy Spirit. Anyone who does not have the Holy Spirit does not belong to God.

Romans 8:10-11:
And if Christ be in you, the body is dead because of sin; but the Spirit is life because of righteousness. But if the Spirit of him that raised up Jesus from the dead dwell in you, he that raised up Christ from the dead shall also quicken your mortal bodies by his Spirit that dwelleth in you.

314

Here is the quickening power of God through the Spirit. This is the reason why I previously stated that religion is different than receiving the spirit. When we are quickened by God's Spirit it means that God's Spirit goes into our bodies and God begans to live and dwell in us, then we will not fulfill the lust of the flesh. Religion will never do this. Let us look at **Romans 8:13:**

For if ye live after the flesh, ye shall die: but if ye through the Spirit do mortify (kill) the deeds of the body, ye shall live.

Therefore the Holy Spirit is able to kill the deeds (works) of the body. You may ask what are the deeds of body? The word of God found in the book of Galatians will show us the deeds of the body, as Apostle Paul has written about "the works of the flesh." Let us read:

Galatians 5:17-21
For the flesh lusteth against the Spirit, and the Spirit against the flesh: and these are contrary the one to the other: so that ye cannot do the things that ye would. But if ye be led of the Spirit, ye are not under the law.[The law of sin.] *Now the works of flesh are manifest, (made known or revealed) which are these; Adultery, fornication, uncleanness, lasciviousness, Idolatry, witchcraft, hatred, variance, emulations, wrath, strife, seditions, heresies, Envyings, murders, drunkenness, revellings and such like: of the which I tell you before, as I have also told you in time past, that they which do such things shall not inherit the kingdom of God.*

The great excuse for fulfilling the lust of the flesh is

"after all, I am only human." However, God says whosoever does these thing (written above) shall not inherit the kingdom of God. This includes **liars,** practitioners of **witchcraft, astrologists, palm readers, tea readers, Reverend Mothers, soothsayers**, etc. Many people like to visit the **fortune tellers** believing nothing is wrong with the practice. All these things are an abomination in the sight of God. These are the works of the flesh. Remember **Galatians 5:21:** *"those who do such things such not inherit the kingdom of God."*

Chapter 63

THE HOLY SPIRIT IS A BAPTIZER

In the book of Galatians, Apostle Paul shows the church that the Holy Spirit is also a baptizer.

Galatians 3:26
For ye are all the children of God by faith in Christ Jesus. For as many of you as have been baptized into Christ (baptized with the Holy Ghost) have put on Christ. There is neither Jew nor Greek, there is neither bond nor free, there is neither male nor female: for ye are all one in Christ Jesus. And if ye be Christ's, then are ye Abraham's seed, and heirs according to the promise.

After we are baptized with the Holy Spirit, something takes place. We no longer look at each other as a Jew, as a male or a female because we become spiritual beings. We are still walking in a fleshly body, but it is the Spirit of God on the inside having control. We may receive the water baptism as many times as we wish, however, it will not take away the fact that we are Jew, male or female. But through the Holy Spirit we are known by God and we know him. It is the Holy Spirit that changes us and washes away the filthiness of the flesh. As Apostle Paul stated:

11 Corinthians 7:1:
Having therefore these promises, dearly beloved, let us cleanse ourselves from all filthiness of the flesh and spirit,

perfecting holiness in the fear of God.

It is the Holy Ghost that makes us Holy.

BAPTIZED INTO THE BODY

Let us go to **I Corinthians** where we will continue to see the Holy Ghost presented as a baptizer.

I Corinthians 12:12
For as the body is one, and hath many members, and all the members of that one body, being many, are one body: so also is Christ. For by one Spirit are we all baptized into one body, whether we be Jews or Gentiles, whether we be bond of free, and have been all made to drink into one Spirit. For the body is not one member, but many. If the foot shall say, Because I am not the hand, I am not of the body; is it therefore not of the body?

As the writer states, there is one body (the body of Christ) and we are all baptized into that one body. Some say when we are baptized in water, we put on Christ. That is not so. Just as we have a natural body which has many members to it, so in the natural, in the spiritual. We have arms, legs, nose, mouth eyes, etc. We are members of one body. Remember Jesus said:

St. Matthew: 5:29-30.
And if thy right eye offend thee, pluck it out, and cast it from thee: for it is profitable for thee that one of thy members should perish, and not that thy whole body should be cast into hell. And if thy right hand offend thee, cut it off, and cast if from thee: for it is profitable for thee that

one of thy members should perish, and not that thy whole body should be cast into hell.

Just as there is a natural body there is a spiritual body with many members. That spiritual body is Christ's and it has many members. This is just how God deals with us in his word.

Chapter 64

THE HOLY SPIRIT
CAN BE TAKEN AWAY FROM US

Let us now go over to the **51st** division of **Psalms**. We must realize that the Holy Spirit can be taken away from us, although Apostle Paul tell us in **Ephesians 4:30**, *"whereby ye are sealed unto the day of redemption."*

We are! However, that seal can be broken. It is just like Christmas. We can have a package neatly wrapped and sealed and it says, " do not open until Christmas." But we can break that seal before Christmas and many of us have.

Let us now read **Psalms 51:11:**

Cast me not away from thy presence; and take not thy holy spirit from me. Restore unto me the joy of thy salvation; and uphold me with thy free spirit.

This is King David crying out unto God. This should be all of our cries. We that have received the Holy Spirit should ask God to keep us and let us not lose the blessing he has blessed us with.

Apostle Paul also recognized that if he did not do the will of God, he, too, would be a castaway.

I Corinthians 9:27
But I keep under my body, and bring it into subjection; lest that by any means, when I have preached to others, I myself should be a castaway.

Thus far we have been looking at the movement of the Holy Spirit. We studied how He moves in part, goes along with, comes upon and other various ways, according to the Scripture.

PART XIV

THE MINISTRY OF

JOHN THE BAPTIST

The thing I desire to write about at this time is the ministry of John the Baptist. Previously, I have touched on it, however, I find it important to deal more extensively regarding John the Baptist's ministry. So many of our preachers, teachers, scholars, etc., seem to get away from the message of John the Baptist. But, you cannot understand or see the plan of salvation without studying his ministry. I advise every preacher, teacher, every baptized believer and all those who are studying the Bible and desire to know the plan of salvation to study and understand the ministry of this man. It is very important. We know when people say, "You must be saved" or "You must be born again," they are talking about your salvation. My experience has been, that I seldom hear them mention the ministry of John the Baptist. He was the forerunner of Jesus Christ and one of the most important men in our Bible. Jesus attested to this when he made this statement:

St. Luke 7:28.

For I say unto you, Among those that are born of women there is not a greater prophet than John the Baptist: but he that is least in the kingdom of God is greater than he.

Jesus was speaking about Himself, when He said:
He that is least in the kingdom of God is greater than he.

Jesus is greater than John. I realize that many say, "he that calleth on the Lord shall be saved," however, what is the word speaking about? As we go to the Scriptures to find out, keep in mind John's ministry, the word, the time, the era and what he spoke regarding Jesus Christ.

Chapter 65

THE PROPHECY OF THE FORERUNNER

Malachi 3:1-3:
Behold, I will send my messenger, and he shall prepare the way before me: and the Lord, whom ye seek, shall suddenly come to his temple, even the messenger of the covenant, whom ye delight in: behold, he shall come, saith the Lord of hosts. But who may abide the day of his coming? and who shall stand when he appeareth? for he is like a refiner's fire, and like fullers' soap. And he shall sit as a refiner and purifier of silver: and he shall purify the sons of Levi and purge them as gold and silver, that they may offer unto the LORD an offering in righteousness.

This is John the Baptist, the messenger, the forerunner, who is going before Jesus Christ Jesus said of him:

St. Luke 7:27.
This is he, of whom it is written, Behold, I send my messenger before thy face, which shall prepare thy way before thee.

HIS HERITAGE
The Bible records the birth of John the Baptist and his mission:

St. Luke 1:13-17
But the angel said unto him, Fear not Zacharias: [John's father] for thy prayer is heard; and thy wife Elizabeth shall

bear thee a son, and thou shalt call his name John. And thou shalt have joy and gladness; and many shall rejoice at his birth. For he sahll be great in the sight of the Lord, and shall drink neither wine nor strong drink: and he shall be filled with the Holy Ghost, even from his mother's womb. And many of the children of Israel shall he turn to the Lord their God. And he shall go before him in the spirit and power of Elias, to turn the hearts of the fathers to the children, and the disobedient to the wisdom of the just; to make ready a people prepared for the Lord.

As the Scripture stated, John came in the spirit and power of Elijah, a hairy man girt about with a girdle of leather about his loins.

II Kings 1:8.
He was a hairy man and girt with a girdle of leather about his loins.

Therefore, John the Baptist was dressed like him, and he was in the Spirit of Elijah. The Spirit of God was not only upon John, but the Spirit was in John. When Mary ran and told her cousin Elizabeth about the salutation from the angel, that she should bring forth a child the baby leaped in Elizabeth's womb. That baby was John the Baptist. Let us read:

St. Luke 1:36-37, 41.
And, behold, thy cousin Elisabeth, she hath also conceived a son in her old age: and this the sixth month with her, [This verifies a six month age difference between John the Baptist and Jesus Christ] *who was called barren. For with God nothing shall be impossible. And it came to pass, that,*

when Elisabeth heard the salutation of Mary, the babe leaped in her womb: and Elisabeth was filled with the Holy Ghost.

HIS MISSION

As we return to **Malachi 3:2-3** the word is asking, *But who may able to abide the day of his coming? and who shall be able to stand when he appeareth? for he is like a refiner's fire, and like fullers' soap: And he shall sit as a refiner and purifier of silver: and he shall purify the sons of Levi, and purge them as gold and silver, that may offer unto the Lord an offering in righteousness.*

The sons of Levi are of the Priesthood which came from the tribe of Levi. The priest miserably failed God in days gone by. They were taken from among men to minister unto the people the things pertaining to God as recorded in **Hebrews.**

Hebrews 5:-1-4:

For every high priest taken from among men is ordained for men in things pertaining to God, that he may offer both gifts and sacrifices for sins: Who can have compassion on the ignorant, and on them that are out of the way; for that he himself also is compassed with infirmity. And by reason hereof he ought, as for the people, so also for himself to offer sins. And no man taketh this honour unto himself, but he that is called of God, as was Aaron.

Malachi is informing us that the Lord would come into the temple and purify the priest and his people. He would purge the sons of Levi as silver and gold. God was going to be like a refiner. After this cleansing then they would offer

327

an offering in righteousness. What **Malachi** is saying pertaining to the ministry of John the Baptist, plays a very important part in this study of the Holy Spirit.

HIS MESSAGE UNTO REPENTANCE

Let us again go to **St. Matthew 3rd chapter**. It is very important. Previously, we have read this chapter, however, it is very important to broaden our knowledge. With this reading, keep in mind that John the Baptist, the forerunner of Jesus Christ, was full of the Holy Ghost from his mother's womb.

St. Matthew 3:1-9:

In those days came John the Baptist, preaching in the wilderness of Judea, And saying, Repent ye: for the kingdom of heaven is at hand. For this is he that was spoken of by the prophet Esaias, [Isaiah] *saying, The voice of one crying in the wilderness, Prepare ye the way of the Lord, make his paths straight. And the same John had his raiment of camel's hair, and a leather girdle about his loins; and his meat was locusts(these were bugs, a diet of many of the poor) and wild honey. Then went out to him Jersusalem, and all Judea, and all the region round about Jordan, And were baptized of him in Jordan confessing their sins. But when he saw many of the Pharisees and Sadducees* [These were the church folks in those days.] *come to his baptism,* [Notice John said his baptism*] he said unto them, O generation of vipers* [snakes] *who hath warned you to flee from the wrath to come? Bring forth therefore fruits* [works] *meet for repentance. And think not to say within yourselves, We have Abraham to our father: for I say unto you, that God is able of these stones to raise up children unto Abraham.*

John is letting them know not to say that they had Abraham as their father. They were trusting in the righteousness of Abraham and the righteousness of Abraham could not get any of them into heaven. The same is true for today. The righteousness of our mother, father will not get us into heaven. Salvation is a personal thing. The Pharisees and the Sadducees were trusting in Abraham and the law of Moses. John is commanding them to bring works that God can approve of for repentance.

St. Matthew 3:10:
And now also the axe is laid unto the root of the trees: therefore, every tree which bringeth not forth good fruit is hewn down, and cast into the fire. I indeed baptize you with water unto repentance: but he that cometh after me is mightier than I, whose shoes I am not worthy to bear: he shall baptize you with the Holy Ghost and with fire: Whose fan is in his hand, and he will throughly purge his floor, and gather his wheat into the garner; but he will burn up the chaff with unquenchable fire.

I MUST DECREASE-HE MUST INCREASE
As great as man as John the Baptist was, he recognized that he was not even worthy to pick up Jesus' shoe. Jesus Christ is the son of the living God. **St. Mark 1:7** states: *"There cometh one mightier than I after me* [meaning Jesus Christ], *the latchet of whose shoes I am not worthy to stoop down and unloose."*

John was a great man. The Holy Ghost prophesied these word concerning John the Baptist:

St. Luke 1:76.
And thou, child, shalt be called the prophet of the Highest:

329

for thou shalt go before the face of the Lord to prepare his ways.

However, John knew that he must decrease. The last testimony of John the Baptist included this statement:

St. John 3:30.
He must increase, but I must decrease.

Chapter 66

JESUS BAPTIZED BY JOHN

Let us continue with **St. Matthew 3:13-15**:

Then cometh Jesus from Galilee to Jordan unto John, to be baptized of him. But John forbad him, saying, I have need to be baptized of thee, and comest thou to me?

In other words, John is asking Jesus, how is it that you are coming to me to receive this ritual of baptism for the remission of sins although you have no sins. I need your baptism; the baptism of the Holy Ghost. Remember John was already filled with the Holy Ghost from his mother's womb. Therefore, he is actually saying to Jesus, I need more of your baptism.

And Jesus answering said unto him, Suffer it to be so now: for thus it becometh us to fulfill all righteousness. Then he suffered him.

To fulfill all righteousness, meaning the Scriptures must be fulfilled, John made these two statements which must be fulfilled:
St. John 1:31; 33-34
And I knew him not: but that he should be made manifest to Israel, therefore, am I come baptizing with water. And I knew him not: but he that sent me to baptize with water, the same said unto me, Upon whom thou shalt see the Spirit descending, and remaining on him, the same is he which

331

*baptizeth with the Holy Ghost. And I saw and bare record
that this is the Son of God.*

Again, I will be repetitious in saying that this was
prophecy, the word of God and righteousness being
fulfilled.

Chapter 67

JESUS AND HIS HOLY GHOST BAPTISM

Let us continue with **St. Matthew 3:16-17:**

And Jesus, when he was baptized went straightway out of the water: and, lo, the heavens were opened unto him, and he saw the Spirit of God descending like a dove, and lighting upon him: And, lo, a voice from heaven, saying, This is my beloved Son, in whom I am well pleased.

The Holy Ghost descended on Jesus in the form of a dove and Jesus was not only baptized with the water baptism, but also by the Holy Ghost. Remember what John the Baptist said about Jesus' baptism:

St. Mark 1:8.
I indeed have baptized you with water: but He shall baptize you with the Holy Ghost.

This was Jesus' baptism, yet many are putting it to the water.

Romans 6:4-10
Therefore we are buried with him by baptism into death: that like as Christ was raised up from the dead by the glory of the Father, even so we also should walk in the newness of life. For if we have been planted together in the likeness of his death, we shall be also in the likeness of his resurrection: Knowing this, that our old man is crucified

with him, that the body of sin might be destroyed, that henceforth we should not serve sin. For he that is dead is freed from sin.

The body is dead in our sins and trespasses without the Holy Spirit and alive with the Holy Spirit and is free the practice of sin.

Now if we be dead with Christ, we believe that we shall also live with him: Knowing that Christ being raised from the dead dieth no more; death hath no more dominion over him. For in that he died, he died unto sin once; but that he liveth, he liveth unto God.

I am not talking about church doctrine. Neither am I concerned with church doctrine. However, I am concerned with the word of God. In order to get a good understanding of Romans 6th chapter, you must remember **I Corinthians 1:10-17,** as to why Apostle Paul was thanking God that he was not sent to baptize in the water. Then hold on to what John said about the two baptisms. If you keep these things in mind the **16th** chapter of **St. Mark** will give you a clear picture of what Jesus is saying. You can be baptized in water all you desire to but it will never do for you what is recorded in the gospel according to St. Mark:

St. Mark 16:16-18.

He that believeth and is baptized shall be saved; [This is not the water baptism] *but he that believeth not shall be damned. And these signs shall follow them that believe; In my name shall they cast out devils; they shall speak with new tongues, They shall take up serpents: and if they drink any deadly thing, it shall not hurt them: they shall lay hands on the sick, and they shall recover.*

The way to understand the fullness of this portion of Scripture is to keep in mind John the Baptist's testimony along with Jesus saying that "He had a baptism to be baptized with." Tie these together along with **Romans 6th** chapter and you will begin to understand what you have. You will also clearly see what John is saying. You cannot bypass the testimony of John the Baptist and then zero in on other Scriptures. You must keep John the Baptist's testimony before you, when you study the Scriptures.

Let us now go to the book of **Acts.** At this point let us remember the testimony of John the Baptist.

ACTS 1:3-5
To whom he shewed himself alive after his passion by many infallible proofs, being seen of them forty days, and speaking of the things pertaining to the kingdom of God: And being assembled together with them, commanded that they should not depart from Jerusalem, but wait for the promise of the Father, which, saith he, ye have heard of me. For John truly baptized with water; but ye shall be baptized with the Holy Ghost not many days hence.

Did not John say make this same declaration? John baptized with water, but Jesus would baptize with the Holy Ghost.

Also we have the Scriptures of James and John where one wanted to sit on the right hand of Jesus in heaven and the other on his left hand.

St. Mark 10:35-40.
And James and John, the sons of Zebedee, come unto him,

335

saying, Master, we would that thou shouldest do for us whatsoever we shall desire. And he said unto them, What would ye that I should do for you? They said unto him, Grant unto us that we may sit, one on thy right hand, and the other on thy left hand, in thy glory. But Jesus said unto them, Ye know not what ye ask: can ye drink of the cup that I drink of? and be baptized with the baptism that I am baptized with? And they said unto him, We can. And Jesus said unto them, Ye shall indeed drink of the cup that I drink of; and with the baptism that I am baptized withal shall ye baptized. But to sit on my right hand and on my left hand is not mine to give; but it shall be given to them for whom it is prepared.

We must remember the baptism that Jesus was speaking about is the Holy Ghost baptism which He was baptized with. The cup He was speaking about was His ministry. The disciples were partakers of both; the baptism of Jesus Christ and the ministry of Jesus Christ. All of this is consistent with what John said regarding his ministry and the ministry of Jesus Christ. Jesus let them to know that he could not grant them the authority to sit on the right and/or left because His Father had already chosen the ones that would sit on the right and left. God has the place prepared.

ACTS 2:4

Most of us are familiar with how the Apostles received the Holy Ghost according to the book of **Acts.**

Acts 2:4.
And they were all filled with the Holy Ghost, and began to speak with other tongues, as the Spirit gave them utterance.

If you read the entire **1st** and **2nd** chapter, you will see there were one hundred and twenty in the upper room, including, Mary the mother of Jesus and his biological brethren, the disciples and others.

THE HOLY SPIRIT GIVES YOU POWER

Let me brief you on the following: The one hundred and twenty that came down from the upper room on the day of Pentecost had power. They spoke in tongues as the Spirit gave them utterance. (Read Acts 2nd chapter) Remember tongues are for a sign.

Allow me to now brief you on the ministry of Gideon and his three hundred men. God told Gideon to take his men down to the water and all who lap water like a dog take them along and God would give him the victory. Gideon did as he was instructed and three hundred men got down on their knees and lapped water like a dog. That lapping water with the motion of the tongues represent speaking in tongues. Gideon's three hundred men had power. Let us read from the book of Judges

JUDGES 7:5-7,16, 22

So he [Gideon] brought down the people unto the water: and the Lord said unto Gideon, Everyone that lappeth of the water with his tongue, as a dog lappeth, him shalt thou set by himself; likewise every one that boweth down upon his knees to drink. And the number of them that lapped, putting their hand to their mouth, were three hundred me: but all the rest of the people bowed down upon their knees to drink water. And the Lord said unto Gideon, By the three hundred me that lapped will I save you, and deliver the Midianites into thine hand: and let all the other people go every man unto his place. And he [Gideon] divided the three hundred men into three companies, and he put a trumpet in every man's hand, with empty pitchers, and lamps within the pitchers. And the three hundred blew the trumpets, and the Lord set every man's sword against his fellow, even throughout all the host: and the host fled to Bethshittah in Zererath, and to the border of Abelmeholah, unto Tabbath.

THE POWER IS NOT IN THE WATER

Anyone who takes power of the Holy Ghost and attributes it to the water, minimizes the power of the Holy Ghost. He is not understanding the function of the Holy Ghost. The power of the Holy Spirit must be taken out of the water and put in its proper place. If a particular Scripture is speaking about the water baptism, then keep it in context. Remember the words of Apostle Paul:

II Timothy 2:15:
Study to show thyself approved unto God, a workman that needeth not to be ashamed, rightly dividing the word of truth.

Every time one sees the word baptize in the Scriptures he cannot just assume it is the water. That is not so.

Chapter 68

THE QUESTIONS AND ANSWERS MOST FREQUENTLY DISCUSSED ABOUT THE WATER BAPTISM

OBSERVE:
In order to fully understand the Scriptures one must know the era and place at the time of the writings and whom the writer was referring to. Keep this in mind in answering the following questions.

QUESTION #1: Under what dispensation was the water baptism?
ANSWER: The water baptism was the dispensation of "Law." Although the water baptism took place during the earthly ministry of Jesus Christ, the **6th dispensation of "Grace"** did not come into its fullness of time until the day of Pentecost.

QUESTION #2: Unto whom was the "Water Baptism"? Why?
ANSWER: The water baptism was unto Israel. It was the remission of sins.

QUESTION #3: Please give a few biblical references to the above question and answer.
ANSWER: **Isaiah 40:3:** Foretells the prophecy of John the Baptist and his ministry to Israel. *The voice of him that crieth in the wilderness, Prepare ye the way of the Lord, make straight in the desert a highway for our God.*

The Gospel according to **St. Mark 1:4** records: *John did baptise in the wilderness, and preach the baptism of repentance for the remission of sins.*

The Gospel of **St. Luke 1:16-17** records: *And many of the children of Israel shall he [John] turn to the Lord their God. And he shall go before him in the spirit and power of Elias, to turn the hearts of the fathers to the children, and the disobedient to the wisdom of the just; to make ready a people prepared for the Lord.*

The Gospel according to **St. John 1:31** records: *And I [John] knew him not: but that he should made manifest to Israel, therefore, I am come baptizing with water.*

QUESTION #4   Can The water baptism remit sins? Why?

ANSWER: No! Jesus is the only one able to remit sins. **Hebrews 9:22** says: *and without the shedding of b l o o d there is no remission of sins.* It is the Holy Ghost which cleanses away the filthiness of the flesh.

QUESTION #5   Explain the doctrinal differences brought about concerning the words of Christ in **St. Matthew 3:15**: *Suffer it to be so now: For thus it becometh us to fulfil all righteousness.*

ANSWER   These words were spoken at the time that, Jesus was about to be baptized in the River Jordan by John the Baptist. Jesus had come to fulfill the law and the prophecy **(Isaiah 40:3).** The Scriptures must be fulfilled. Also John would only recognize Jesus because of the baptism. *Upon whom thou shalt see the Spirit descending and remaining on him the same is he which baptizeth with the Holy Ghost.*

QUESTION #6   Did Jesus baptize with water? State your proof.

ANSWER: No! My proof can be found in **St. John 4:1-2:** *The Pharisees had heard that Jesus himself made and baptized more disciples than John. Though Jesus himself baptized not, but his disciples.*

QUESTION #7   Relate the ministry of Jesus Christ regarding the water baptism, to the ministry of Apostle Paul. What similaries do you find?

ANSWER: Just as with Jesus, Apostle Paul's ministry was not focused on the water baptism. (Although he did baptize a few). Apostle Paul stated in **I Corinthians 1:14-17** *I thank God that I baptized none of you, but Crispus and Gaius, Lest any should say that I had baptized in mine own name. For Christ sent me not to baptize, but to preach the gospel.*

QUESTION #8:   What was Apostle Paul trying to get the church at Corinth to see (**1 Cor.1:14**) regarding the water baptism?

ANSWER: The water baptism has brought about much division. The church was more into following human leadership and emphasis was being placed on whose name they were baptized in thus dividing the body.

QUESTION #9:   What was Apostles Paul's reaction to the disciples he met whom had gone no further than John's baptism?

ANSWER: **Acts 19:6** *And when Paul laid his hands upon them, the Holy Ghost came on them; and they spake with tongues and they prophesied.*

QUESTION #10: What was Jesus' baptism? Please elaborate, using various Scriptures to support your answers.
ANSWER (#1) The Holy Ghost and fire. John the Baptist stated in St. **Matthew 3:11,** *I indeed baptize you with water unto repentance: but he that cometh after me is mightier that I, whose shoes I am not worthy to bear: he shall baptize you with the Holy Ghost, and with fire.*

(#2) According to **St. Matthew 20:22:** Jesus asked his disciples, *Are ye able to drink of the cup that I shall drink of, and to be baptized with the baptism that I am baptized with.*

(#3) **Acts 1:5** Jesus said: *For John truly baptized with water but ye shall be baptized with the Holy Ghost not many days hence.* On the day of Pentecost they were then baptized with Jesus' baptism as he foretold them in the previous Scripture(s).

QUESTION #11: What affect did it have upon the ministries of the disciples?
ANSWER: **ACTS 1:8:** *But ye shall receive power, after that the Holy Ghost is come upon you: and ye shall be witnesses unto me both in Jerusalem, and in all Judea, and in Samaria, and unto the uttermost part of the earth.*

QUESTION #12: Which baptism was Jesus speaking of in St. **Mark 16:16:** *He that believeth and is baptized shall be saved; but he that believeth not shall be damned.*
ANSWER: Jesus was speaking of *His* baptism, which is the Holy Ghost baptism.

QUESTION #13 According to the gospel of **St. Matthew 28:19,** Jesus commanded his disciples to: *Go ye therefore and teach all nations, baptizing them in the name* *of the Father, and of the Son, the Holy Ghost.* What actually was Jesus commanding?

ANSWER: Jesus' command was that his disciples go and teach with the emphasis being on the Holy Ghost baptism. The same as with **St. Mark 16:15.**

QUESTION 14: Please give other Biblical references regarding the Holy Ghost baptism.

ANSWER: We must refer to **Romans 6:3-4:** *Know ye not that so many of us as were baptized into Jesus Christ were baptized into his death? Therefore we are buried with him by baptism into death: that like as Christ was raised up from the dead by the glory of the Father, even so we also should walk in newness of life.*

We must also read **Colossians 2:12:** *Buried with him in baptism, wherein also ye are risen with him through the faith of the operation of God, who hath raised him from the dead.*

We cannot neglect **Galatians 3:27**: *For as many of you as have been baptized into Christ have put on Christ.* (Note: It is baptized into the body of Christ, **NOT** baptized into the Holy Ghost.

QUESTION #15: Apostle Peter referred to the Holy Ghost as a gift. Keeping in mind the context of the Scriptures, summarize your thoughts on this matter.

ANSWER: Keeping in mind the context of the Scripture(s) one must realize that "gift" simply means unconditional favor of God. Erroneous teachings are applied when one sees the Holy Ghost as just a gift and not Jesus' baptism, Emphasis is then placed on the water and the Holy Ghost just being a little addition. The Bible (**Ephesians 4:5**) clearly declares, **"One Lord,** [Jesus] **One Faith**

343

[Holiness]and **One baptism** [the Holy Ghost]." There is a doctrine that expresses the one baptism (stated above) is the water baptism in Jesus name only, building a baptismal foundation on Apostle Peter. However, when God sent Peter to the household of Cornelius, the Holy Ghost fell on them which heard the word. (**Read Acts 10:44**) Peter then remembered the word of the Lord. *For John indeed baptized with water; but ye shall be baptized with the Holy Ghost not many days hence.* Acts 1:5

QUESTION #16: Now that you understand the baptisms, do you perceive any problems with those desiring to be baptized in the water.

ANSWER: No, not unless one feels that he has to go no further. Some feel inadequate without the water baptism. Therefore, let him be baptized. But I'd make sure they know that without the Holy Ghost, there is no salvation.

PART XV

THOU ART THE CHRIST

Chapter 69

APOSTLE PETER'S REVELATION

Let us go futher into the Scriptures regarding the ministry of John the Baptist.

St. Matthew 16:13-18.

When Jesus came in the coasts of Ceasarea Philippi, he asked his disciples, saying, Whom do men say that I the Son of man am? And they said, Some say that thou art John the Baptist: some, Elias; and others, Jermias, or one of the prophets. He saith unto them, But whom say ye that I am? And Simon Peter answered and said, Thou art the Christ, the Son of the living God; And Jesus answered and said unto him, Blessed art thou, Simon Barjona: for flesh and blood hath not revealed it unto thee, but my Father which is in heaven. And I say also unto thee, That thou art Peter, and upon this rock I will build my church; and the gates of hell shall not prevail against it. And I will give unto thee the keys of the kingdom of heaven: and whatsoever thou shalt bind on earth shall be bound in heaven: and whatsoever thou shalt loose on earth shall be loosed in heaven.

It was the Holy Spirit that revealed this thing unto Peter. As I have stated the Holy Spirit is a revealer. This is why Jesus called him the Spirit of truth.

St. John 16:13
Howbeit when he, the Spirit of truth, is come, he will guide

you into all truth:

The Spirit of truth will bring out the truths of God to let us to know the spiritual things of God.

UPON THIS ROCK
This revelation came unto Peter.
St. Matthew 16:17-18
Jesus said: *Blessed art thou, Simon Barjona: for flesh and blood hath not revealed it unto thee, but my Father which is in heaven. And I say also unto thee, That thou art Peter, and upon this rock I will build my church; and the gates of hell shall not prevail against it.*

We know that the Scripture says that upon this rock He was to build his church. It was upon Peter's revelation and faith. The rock is Jesus. If you would read the Epistle of Peter, you will see how Peter clearly made it known that the rock was Jesus Christ. Peter also referred to Jesus as a rock of offence:

I Peter 2:8.
And a stone of stumbling, and a rock of offence, even to them which stumble at the word, being disobedient:

Apostle Paul also speaks of rock that followed the children of Israel in the wilderness and that rock was Jesus:

I Corinthians 10:4.
And did all drink the same spiritual drink: for they drank of that spiritual Rock that followed them: and that Rock was Christ.

Being repetitious, I write unto you again. Jesus is

building the church upon Peter's profession of faith not upon Peter the man.

St. Matthew 16:16
Thou art the Christ, the Son of the living God

If the church had been built upon Peter the church would have failed. The word of God states that Christ is the head of the body; His body is the church.

I Corinthians 12:13
For by one Spirit are we all baptized into one body.

PETER GIVEN THE KEYS TO THE KINGDOM
Remember the Lord gave Peter the keys to the kingdom.

St. Matthew 16:18-19
And I say also unto thee, That thou art Peter, and upon this rock I will build my church; and the gates of hell shall not prevail against it. And I will give unto thee the keys of the kingdom of heaven: and whatsoever thou shalt bind on earth shall be bound in heaven: and whatsoever thou shalt loose on earth shall be loosed in heaven.

On the day of Pentecost Apostle Peter stood and preached one of the most powerful sermons ever recorded in the Bible.

ACTS 2:37-38
Now when they heard this, they were pricked in their heart, and said unto Peter and to the rest of the apostles, Men and brethren, what shall we do? Then Peter said unto them, Repent, and be baptized every one of you in the name of

349

Jesus Christ for the remission of sins, and ye shall receive the gift of the Holy Ghost.

The Holy Ghost is a baptism. Apostle Peter called it a gift, because there is no price on the Holy Ghost. We receive the Holy Spirit freely. Keep in context what I am saying. As the Scripture states:

I Corinthians 6:20.
For ye are brought with a price: therefore glorify God in your body, and in your spirit, which are God's.

Therefore, I am not minimizing the price Christ paid on the cross. Jesus paid it all.

Chapter 70

THE HOUSEHOLD OF CORNELIUS

Let us go to **Acts 10:1-6**.

There was a certain man in Caesarea called Cornelius, a centurion of the band called the Italian band. A devout man, and one that feared God with all his house, which gave much alms to the people, and prayed to God alway. He saw in a vision evidently about the ninth hour of the day and angel of God coming in to him, and saying unto him, Cornelius. And when he looked on him, he was afraid, and said, What is it Lord? And he said unto him, Thy prayers and thine alms are come up for a memorial before God. And now send men to Joppa, and call for one Simon, whose surname is Peter: He lodgeth with one Simon a tanner, whose house is by the sea side; he shall tell thee what thou oughtest to do.

So many times, people say "I am saved." Actually they have been convinced by someone because they have repeated the sinner's prayer. However, here is a man that prayed to God always. He was a very devout and giving man. He was a man that loved God and the people. However, he was not saved. He still had to hear the gospel preached to him. Therefore, I ask, how is it that many or our church leaders are making salvation so easy? All you have to do come up and repeat the sinner's prayer and then you are saved. The Lord is showing Cornelius that he must send for Peter and Peter will tell him what he ought to do. Cornelius put all his love toward God. He is the first

351

Gentile to receive the baptism of the Holy Spirit. Let us continue in **Acts 10:17-22**:

Now while Peter doubted in himself what this vision which he had seen should mean, behold, the men which were sent from Cornelius had made inquiry for Simon's house, and stood before the gate. And called, and asked whether Simon, which surnamed Peter, were lodge there. While Peter thought on the vision, the Spirit said unto him, Behold, three men seek thee. Arise therefore, and get thee down, and go with them doubting nothing: for I have sent them. Then Peter went down to the men which were sent unto him from Cornelius: and said, Behold, I am he whom ye seek: what is the cause wherefore ye are come? And they said, Cornelius the centurion, a just man, and one that feareth God, and of good report among all the nation of the Jews, was warned from God by an holy angel to send for thee into his house and to hear words of thee.

Peter, being a good Jew, would not go to a Gentile house. However, the Holy Ghost directed him to go. Again we witness the working of the Holy Spirit. Therefore Peter went, as instructed doubting nothing. However, before Peter was to go God fixed him up real good. Acts records the vision which God showed unto Peter before his encounter with Cornelius. God had to prepare Peter, because Peter was a good and faithful Jew and Cornelius was a Gentile. Therefore, God dealt with the heart and mind of Peter.

ACTS 10:9-16

On the morrow, as they went on their journey, and drew nigh unto the city, Peter went up upon the housetop to pray about the sixth hour: And he became very hungry and would have eaten: but while they made ready, he fell into a trance. And saw heaven opened, and certain vessel descending unto him, as it had been a great sheet knit at the four corners, and let down to the earth: Wherein were all manner of fourfooted beasts, of the earth, and wild beasts, and creeping things, and fowls of the air. And there came a voice to him, Rise, Peter; kill and eat. But Peter said, Not so, Lord: for I have never eaten any thing that is common or unclean And the voice spake unto him again the second time, What God hath cleansed, that call not thou common. This was done thrice: and the vessel was received up again into heaven.

The Lord was letting Peter know He had cleansed the Gentiles. (Heathen men without God). Therefore Peter, obedient to the heavenly vision, began to preach:

ACTS 10:34-36

Then Peter opened his mouth, and said, Of a truth I perceive that God is no respecter of persons: But in every nation he that feareth him, and worketh righteousness, is accepted with him. The word which God sent unto the children of Israel, preaching peace by Jesus Christ: (for he is Lord of all).

Chapter 71

THE FIRST SPIRIT-FILLED GENTILES

ACTS 10-44-48

While Peter yet spake with these words, the Holy Ghost fell on all them which heard the word. And they of circumcision which believed were astonished, as many as came with Peter, because that on the Gentiles also was poured out the gift of the Holy Ghost. For they heard them speak with tongues, and magnify God. Then answered Peter, Can any man forbid water, that these should not be baptized, which have received the Holy Ghost as well as we? And he commanded them to be baptized in the name of the Lord. Then prayed they him to tarry certain days.

This Scripture as well as others discredit the doctrine of not being able to receive the Holy Ghost until you receive the water baptism. I have witnessed this many times in my ministry. Many people have received the Holy Ghost, even on their hospital beds. I say unto you that God can fill a man with the Holy Ghost in the desert, where there is no water. God can save a man in the desert and on the moon, therefore, if you are saying that man has to have the water baptism in order to be saved, that is not true. It is erroneous doctrine. If God had to depend on water to save a man we would be in mighty bad shape. In many parts of this world water is scarce. Therefore, a lack of water does not stop God. Again, I repeat that God can save a man anywhere. That is what he did with Cornelius and his household.

Let us go futher into the book of Acts where Peter is now rehearsing the matter.

ACTS 11:13
And he shewed us how he had seen an angel in his house, which stood and said, unto him, Send men to Joppa, and call for Simon, whose surname is Peter; Who shall tell thee words, whereby thou and all thy house shall be saved.

As I have stated, people take salvation very lightly, when they say just confess the sinner's prayer and you shall be saved. Look at how this man's prayer had gone up before God as a memorial. All of these things had happened to him, yet he was not saved. Therefore, God sent Peter to tell him words, whereby he and his household would be saved.

Acts 11:15-18.
And as I began to speak, the Holy Ghost fell on them, as on us at the beginning. Then remembered I the word of the Lord, how that he said, John indeed baptize with water; but ye shall be baptized with the Holy Ghost. Forasmuch then as God gave them the gift as he did unto us, who believed on the Lord Jesus Christ; what was I, that I could withstand God? When they heard these things, they held their peace, and glorified God, saying, Then hath God also to the Gentile granted repentance unto life.

We see that Cornelius received the baptism of the Holy Ghost for the saving of his soul.

Hebrews 12:14
Follow peace with all men, and holiness, without which no

356

man shall see the Lord:

The word of God lets us know that the body is dead without the spirit and if Christ be in us, He will quicken our mortal bodies.

Romans 8:10-11:
And if Christ be in you, the body is dead because of sin; but the Spirit is life because of righteousness. But if the Spirit of him that raised up Jesus from the dead dwell in you, he that raised up Christ from the dead shall also quicken your mortal bodies by his Spirit [Holy Ghost] that dwelleth in you.

Also in **Ephesians 2:18:**
For through him we both have access by one Spirit unto the Father.

It is by the Holy Spirit that we have access unto God. Remember what Jesus told the woman at the well.

St. John 4:24.
God is a Spirit: and they that worship him must worship him in spirit and in truth.

Chapter 72

MANY MEMBERS IN ONE BODY

BY ONE SPIRIT

Let us now go over to **1 Corinthians.** Keep in mind that we are still dealing with the ministries of John the Baptist, his water baptism; Jesus Christ and His Holy Ghost baptism.

I CORINTHIANS. 12:12-14
For as the body is one, and hath many members, and all the members of that one body, being many are one body: so also is Christ. For by one Spirit are we all baptized into one body, whether we be Jews or Gentiles, whether we be bond or free; and have been all made to drink into one Spirit. For the body is not one member, but many.

This is the only way we can get into Christ. We must be baptized by the Holy Spirit into his body; not baptized into the Holy Ghost, but baptized into the body of Christ.

KEEPING THE UNITY OF THE SPIRIT

Let us go to **Ephesians 4:1-6:**
I therefore, the prisoner of the Lord, beseech you that ye walk worthy of the vocation wherewith ye are called, With all lowliness and meekness, with longsuffering, forbearing one another in love; Endeavouring to keep the unity of the Spirit in the bond of peace. There is one body, and one

Spirit, even as ye are called in one hope of your calling.
One Lord, one faith, one baptism. One God and Father of
all, who is above all, and through all, and in you all.

We must keep the unity of the spirit. It is amazing how
so many people read this and yet when it comes to the
baptism, they throw two in there constantly.

THERE ARE CONTENTIONS AMONG YOU

One baptism, what is Apostle Paul writing about? Let's
see Paul's view on "One Lord, One faith and One baptism" in
I Corinthians 1:10: Very seldom, if at all, will you hear this
preached. I have only heard one man, other than myself preach
this Scripture. I am not saying that someone else has not
preached it. I have not heard it. Let us read and see what
Apostle Paul is saying to the church:

I Corinthians 1:10-17
Now I beseech you, brethren, by the name of our Lord
Jesus Christ, that ye all speak the same thing, and that
there be no divisions among you; but that ye be perfectly
joined together in the same mind and in the same judgment.
For it has been declared unto me of you my brethren, by
them which are of the house of Chloe, that there are
contentions among you. Now I say, that every one of you
saith, I am of Paul: and I of Apollos; and I of Cephas; and
I of Christ. Is Christ divided? was Paul crucified for you?
or were ye baptized in the name of Paul? I thank God that
I baptized none of you, but Crispus and Gaius: Lest any
should say that I had baptized in mine own name. And I
baptized also the household of Stephanas: besides I know
not whether I baptized any other. For Christ sent me not to

baptize, but to preach the gospel: not with wisdom of words, lest the cross of Christ should be made of none effect.

DIVISIONS AMONG THE PEOPLE

There were divisions among the people. They were all talking about the water baptism and we have the same thing today. The churches are arguing about which way you should be baptized. Thank God if you are baptized in the name of the Father, Son and the Holy Ghost.

According to **ACTS 2:38:**
Then Peter said unto them, Repent, and be baptized every one of you in the name of Jesus Christ for the remission of sins, and ye shall receive the gift of the Holy Ghost.

Remember Apostle Peter spoke these words and it is all Bible. When the one hundred and twenty came down from upper room, and Peter said these words unto those that were pricked in there heart, asking, Men and brethren, "What shall we do? Apostle Peter was speaking to all Jews on the day of Pentecost. He carried on what John said about the baptism and not what Jesus said. Apostle Peter called it a gift. It is a gift, meaning that we receive the Holy Ghost unconditionally. However, the Holy Ghost is Jesus' baptism. If you go to the Book of Acts 10th and 11th chapters, you will see where Apostle Peter witnesses the Holy Ghost falling on the first Gentiles converts without the water baptism. Then he remembered the words of the Lord. Let us read where Apostle Peter was rehearsing the matter. (You must also read Acts Chapter 10.)

Acts 11:15

As I began to speak, the Holy ghost fell on them, as on us at the beginning. Then remembered I the word of the Lord, how that he said John indeed baptized with water; but ye shall be baptized with the Holy Ghost. Forasmuch then as God gave them the like gift as he did unto us, who believed on the Lord Jesus Christ; what was I, that I could withstand God. When they heard these things, they held their peace, and glorified God, saying, Then hath God also to the Gentiles granted repentance unto life.

Before God gave Peter this vision/revelation, Peter was lacking understanding. Therefore, I write unto you do not let people trouble you or upset you as to how you were baptized. The most important thing is that you are baptized, whether it is in the name of the Father, Son and Holy Ghost or whether it is in Jesus name. If you are sprinkled, that is not Biblical. You should be submerged. The most important of all is that you receive the Holy Ghost.

Read again Apostle Paul's writing:

I CORINTHIANS 1:14

I thank God that I baptized none of you, but Crispus and Gaius: Lest any should say that I had baptized in mine own name.

In the 19th chapter of the Book of Acts, Apostle Paul did baptize some and layed his hands on them and they received the Holy Ghost. Nevertheless, Apostle Paul is thanking God that he baptized very few. Paul was not one to put the emphasis on the water baptism. Now if Paul is not the one to put the emphasis on the water baptism as part of your salvation then let us go to Romans 6th chapter and see why, Apostle Paul being the writer, many of our leaders are putting his writing on the water baptism.

Romans 6:1-4

What shall we say then? Shall we continue in sin, that grace may abound? God forbid. How shall we that are dead to sin, live any longer therein? Know ye not, that so many of us as were baptized into Jesus Christ were baptized into his death? Therefore, we are buried with him by baptism into death: that like as Christ was raised up from the dead by the glory of the Father, even so we also should walk in newness of life.

PART XVI

THE WALK IN THE SPIRIT

Chapter 73

THE SPIRIT GIVES LIFE

THE LETTER KILLETH

II Corinthians 3:6
Who also have made us able ministers of the new testament; not of the letter, but of the spirit: for the letter killeth, but the spirit giveth life.

The letter, as Apostle Paul called it, was the law. The letter (Law) did kill. When the Law came into effect, men died. No man was justified by the Law. The Law was a hard school master. The law said:

Exodus 21:23-24.
And if any mischief follow, then thou shalt give life for life. Eye for eye, tooth for tooth, hand for hand, foot for foot.

If a man wanted to get rid of his wife, according to the Scriptures, all he had to do was give her a writing of divorcement.

DUETERONOMY 24:1.
When a man hath taken a wife, and married her, and it come to pass that she find no favour in his eyes, because he hath found some uncleanness in her: then let him write her a bill of divorcement, and give it in her hand, and send her out of his house.

Jesus even spoke about this in regard to law:

St. Matthew 5:31-32.

It hath been said, Whosoever shall put away his wife, let him give her a writing of divorcement: But I say unto you, That whosoever shall put away his wife, saving for the cause of fornication, causeth her to commit adultery: and whosoever shall marry her that is divorced committeth adultery.

Again I repeat the letter (law) killeth, but the spirit giveth life. Jesus said:

St. John 6:63.

... words that I speak unto you, they are spirit and they are life.

Therefore, the word of God is spirit and it still stands true to this day. Let us go to the book of **Ephesians,** the writings of the Apostle Paul.

Ephesians. 6:10-11

Finally, my brethren, be strong in the Lord, and in the power of his might. Put on the whole armour of God, that ye may be able to stand against the wiles of the devil.

You notice Apostle Paul said, "brethren." This is a Holy spirit-filled church. He is saying unto us to put on the whole armor of God that we may be able to stand against the wiles (methods) of the Devil. How do we put on the whole armor of God. We must do it through the Spirit. Remember we agreed with the word of God saying, by one Spirit are we all baptized into one body. Therefore, we put on the whole armor of God by walking in the Spirit (walking according to God' word) that we might not fulfill the lust of the flesh. Remember, Jesus said:

ACTS 1:8.

But ye shall receive power, after that the Holy Ghost is come upon you: and ye shall be witnesses unto me both in Jerusalem, and in all Judea, and in Samaria, and unto the uttermost part of the earth:

Jesus would not let them leave Jerusalem until they were endued with power from on high.

ST. LUKE 24:49.

And, behold, I send the promise of my Father upon you: but tarry ye in the city of Jerusalem, until ye be endued with power from on high .

The Holy Spirit is our Salvation because we are baptized into Christ and once we are in Christ, as God says, I will not write my law upon plaques anymore, but I will write them upon the hearts of men and I will walk in them and talk in them; they shall be my sons and my daughters.

Chapter 74

GRIEVE NOT THE SPIRIT

Ephesians 4:30-32:
And grieve not the holy Spirit of God, whereby ye are sealed until the day of redemption. Let all bitterness and wrath, and anger, and clamour, and evil speaking, be put away from you with all malice. And be ye kind one to another, tenderhearted, forgiving one another, even as God for Christ's sake hath forgiven you.

Apostle Paul wrote about the love of God shed abroad in our hearts by the Holy Ghost.

ROMANS 5:5
And hope maketh not ashamed; because the love of God is shed abroad in our hearts by the Holy Ghost given unto us.

SEALED UNTO THE DAY OF REDEMPTION

Notice what Apostle Paul said about grieving not the Holy Spirit of God, because we are sealed until the day of redemption. The Holy Spirit is a seal. That is how we are baptized into Christ; Christ in God and we in Christ. Remember in the Book of Job, the Old Testament, how Satan challenged God by saying "Does Job serve you for nought, take the hedge from around him and I will make him curse you to the face." The hedge, as the Bible refers to it, is God's protective force. I definitely know and believe it with all my heart that this hedge (protection) was the Holy Spirit, which is God's power. God protected Job as he went about daily. The Spirit of wisdom was upon Job because he was a wise man. Many came to him to be counseled. The Holy Spirit was shed aboard in his heart. I am not saying the Job was baptized with the Holy Spirit, speaking in tongues as we are. however, again I say in the Old Testament, the Spirit of God strove with men and upon man. The spirit of wisdom was in man. God was very capable in working in Job, although Job was self righteous, but God gave him wisdom and understanding. He was a man of love, because he shared with many. Job had a good report.

THE WORKS OF THE SPIRIT

Let us go to **EPHESIANS 5:9:**
(*For the fruit of the Spirit is in all goodness and righteousness and truth*)

The fruit of the spirit means works. The Spirit has works, just as the flesh has works. The flesh wars on the Spirit, and the Spirit wars on the flesh. There is a great battle going on between the two.

Ephesians 6:12-18:
For we wrestle not against flesh and blood, but against principalities, against powers, against the rulers of the darkness of this world, against spiritual wickedness in high places. Wherefore take unto you the whole armour of God, that ye may be able to withstand in the evil day, and having done all, to stand. Stand therefore, having your loins girt about with truth, [the Holy Spirit is truth, Jesus Christ is

truth] *and having on the breastplate of righteousness: And your feet shod with the preparation of the gospel of peace: Above all taking the shield of faith, wherewith ye shall be able to quench all the fiery darts of the darts of the wicked. And take the helmet of salvation, and the sword of the Spirit, which is the word of God: Praying always with all prayer and supplication in the Spirit, and watching thereunto with all perservance and supplication for all saints;*

We must pray in the Spirit and if we have not the Spirit, how can we pray in the Spirit. Apostle Paul stated that we must be filled with the Spirit.

Ephesians 5:18:
And be not drunk with wine wherein is excess; but be filled with the Spirit;

BY THE GRACE OF GOD

Ephesians 4:7-13
But unto every one of us is given grace according to the measure of the gift of Christ. Wherefore, he saith, When he ascended up on high, he led captivity captive, and gave gifts unto men. (Now that he ascended, what is it but that he also descended first into the lower parts of the earth? He that descended is the same also that ascended up far above all heavens, that he might fill all things.) And he gave some apostles, and some, prophets: and some, evangelists; and some, pastors and teachers. For the pefecting of the saints, for the work of the ministry, for the edifying the body of Christ: Till we all come in the unity of the faith, and of the knowledge of the Son of God, unto a perfect man, unto the

measure of the stature of the fullness of Christ.

God gives gifts unto us and they all come through the Holy Spirit, when God is working, talking and walking in us. When he is able to direct our lives, he is able to work in us to his fullness. The Holy Spirit does an awful lot of work. We cannot diminish the workings of the Holy Spirit because he is always active to strengthen and teach the people of God.

In concluding this chapter, let us remember the words of the Apostle Paul:

ACTS 19:2
Have ye received the Holy Ghost since ye believed?

OTHER DEMONOLOGY BOOKS

Manual On Demonology, Diary of An Exorcist, Author Bishop Roy Bryant, Sr., DD $19.95 (or current price) please include and shipping charges ($3.50) for each book.

Out of Me Went 43 Demons, Author, Evangelist Antoinette Cannaday, $8.95 (or current price) include shipping charges ($3.50) for each book.

VARIOUS TAPES BY BISHOP ROY BRYANT, SR. DD
DEMONOLOGY

Demons Speaking Tape #1	Demons Speaking Tape #2
Demons Speaking Tape #3	Demons Speaking Tape #4

Self-Deliverance
Demonology Workshop - You Are What You Eat -Dietary and Vitamins
Who's In Your Body With You? (6 Tape Series)
Exposing The Enemy From Within-Demon Manifestation
Satan The Motivator (2 Tape Series)
Demons and Their Activities *(Exposing demons through conversation with Bishop Roy Bryant, Sr. and Evangelist Antoinette Cannaday)*
A Minister In Distress *(A young minister's deliverance from homosexuality)*
Expelling Demons From The Home
Satan On The Loose (3 Tape Series)
How To Cast Out Demons (2 Tape Series)
Demonology Prayer Breakfast Teachings

SEMINARS

Heresies	The Holy Spirit (4 Tape Series)
Marriage and Sexuality	The Ministry of Jesus Christ
Was Adam Saved? (2 Tape Series)	Tapes from The Minister's -
Spiritual Gifts	- Training Class

Dsyfunctional Families (Demonology Class Tapes)
The Curse of the Woman (Demonology Class Tapes)

TEACHING TAPES BY EVANG. ANTOINETTE CANNADAY
(You may order the following tapes in a 3-tape series for $17.95 or $6.50 each.)
How Do I Know If I Need Deliverance?
I Have Been Delivered, Now What?
The Abused Women in the Church (Not for Women Only)

EACH TAPE IS $6.50 (OR CURRENT PRICE) PLEASE INCLUDE PRIORITY MAIL POSTAGE FOR YOUR TAPES ($3.20).

THE BIBLE CHURCH OF CHRIST, INC.
Bishop Roy Bryant, Sr., D.D. - Pastor

The Bible Church of Christ
HEADQUARTERS
1358 Morris Avenue,
Bronx, New York 10456
(718) 588-2284 Fax 992-5597

The Bible Church of Christ/
ANNEX
1069 Morris Ave.,
(Corner of 166th Street)
Bronx, New York 10456
(718) 992-4653

The Bible Church of Christ
100 West 2nd Street
(Corner of 8th Avenue
Mount Vernon, New York 10550
(914) 664-4602 Fax 668-6778

The Bible Church of Christ
(In Diamond Acres)
Dagsboro, Delaware 19939
(302) 732-3351

The Bible Church of Christ
1140 Congress Street
Schenectady, New York 12023

THE BIBLE CHURCH OF CHRIST, INC.
THEOLOGICAL INSTITUTES
Dr. Roy Bryant, Sr., - President

THEOLOGICAL INSTITUTE
BRONX,
1358 Morris Avenue,
(Corner of 170th Street)
Bronx, New York 10456
(206) 588-2284

THEOLOGICAL INSTITUTE
100 West 2nd Street
(Corner of 8th Avenue)
Mount Vernon, New York
10550
(914) 664-4602

THEOLOGICAL INSTITUTE
(In Diamond Acres)
Dagsboro, Delaware 19939
(302) 732-3351

COURSES OFFERED: New Converts, Christian Workers, Evangelism, General Bible I & II, Teacher Training, Post Graduate in Theology, Advanced Pedagogy, Spanish, GED, Youth Expression, Josephus, **Demonology** and more.

THE BIBLE CHURCH OF CHRIST
CHRISTIAN BOOKSTORE
1358 Morris Avenue
Bronx, New York 10456
(718) 293-1928